MW00791822

BIBLE CHRONOLOGY

MADE EASY

R*SE
PUBLISHING

Bible Chronology Made Easy
© 2022 Rose Publishing

Published by Rose Publishing
An imprint of Tyndale House Ministries
Carol Stream, Illinois
www.hendricksonrose.com

The *Made Easy* series is a collection of concise, pocket-sized books that summarize key biblical teachings and provide clear, user-friendly explanations to common questions about the Christian faith. Find more *Made Easy* books at www.hendricksonrose.com.

ISBN 978-1-64938-053-1

Contributing authors: Jessica Curiel; Len Woods

Cover and page layout design by Cristalle Kishi

Photos and illustrations used under license from Shutterstock.com.

Printed in the United States of America
010322VP

CONTENTS

THE STORY OF THE BIBLE

Like all stories, the story of the Bible includes a few basic components. There are characters—the men, women, and families that the biblical story is about. There are also the characters of the spiritual realm—angels, demons, and the antagonist Satan. But the main character is God, his Son Jesus, and the Holy Spirit. The setting of the story takes place mainly in the Middle East, Asia, and Europe, though we do get occasional peeks into heaven. And don't forget, all stories include a conflict—a problem to be solved. What the characters do to overcome that problem is the plot of the story.

In the Bible, the conflict happens right at the beginning. God's beloved creatures and beautiful world are ruined by sin. Adam and Eve's rebellion brings the curse of sin and death into their perfect lives and pristine world. What will God do to rescue his rebellious creatures?

Shock of shocks, God handpicks an old, childless couple, Abraham and Sarah, and promises to make them into a great nation and bless the entire world through them! However, God's chosen family often fails to live as he commands. The Old Testament stories feature men and women who sometimes turn their hearts toward God, but other times turn their backs on him. Kingdoms and rulers rise and crumble. The curse of sin is not broken.

Then, after the last book of the Old Testament, nearly four centuries pass. The people of God find themselves at the mercy of foreign powers. They wonder: What about all those divine promises of a glorious future? Where is the Messiah that the prophets talked about?

Enter Jesus. This son born to Mary and Joseph of Nazareth is actually the Messiah promised in the Scriptures. Jesus is the unlikely hero of God's story. And what does Jesus do? He gathers followers. He claims to be divine. He tells people to put their faith in him. After living a sinless life, he willingly suffers an excruciating death on a Roman cross, offering his life as the payment for sin. He then defeats death, walking out of a borrowed grave! His followers take his message of love, forgiveness, and new life to the ends of the earth.

Most stories conclude with a resolution to the problem presented at the outset. Here's what's fascinating about God's story: The Bible's last book—Revelation—tells us that God's ultimate resolution is yet to come. The story isn't over. We get to play a part in God's holy plot to redeem and restore all things through Jesus Christ.

The Bible isn't simply "a bunch of old writings from the past," as some might think. It's the portion of God's story that the prophets and apostles recorded as examples for us (1 Cor. 10:11). Until Jesus returns, we get to add to the great, unfolding story. When Christ returns, he will conclude his two-part mission to vanquish evil and make all things new.

📖 GENESIS

Creation: 6 days; rest on 7th day

◆ Adam and Eve in the garden of Eden

◈ Adamic covenant

The Fall: Sin and death

◆ Adam and Eve expelled from Eden.

◆ Cain kills Abel.

◆ Noah's ark and the flood

◈ Noahic covenant

◆ Tower of Babel

Dates for events before Abraham are unknown.

◈ Abrahamic covenant

Abraham goes to Canaan. 2091 BC

◆ Ishmael is born to Abraham and Hagar.

◆ God destroys Sodom and Gomorrah.

◆ Isaac is born to Abraham and Sarah.

◆ Abraham sends Hagar and Ishmael away.

◆ Abraham is tested by God to sacrifice Isaac.

◆ Death of Sarah

◆ Isaac marries Rebekah.

◆ Esau and Jacob are born.

📖 JOB

◆ Death of Abraham

Jacob deceives Isaac and is given ◆ the blessing of the firstborn.

	2100 BC	2000 BC	1900

Abraham 175 years

Sarah 127 years

Isaac 180 years

Jacob 147 years

Time line dates are approximate.

EXODUS

◆ Jacob marries Leah and Rachel.

  ◆ Jacob has 12 sons.

    ◆ Jacob is renamed "Israel."

    ◆ Jacob and Esau reconcile.

  ◆ Death of Rachel

    ◆ Joseph's brothers sell him into slavery.

      ◆ Death of Isaac

    ◆ Judah and Tamar have a son.

    ◆ Joseph thrown into prison.

  ◆ Joseph is made an official in Egypt.

    ◆ Joseph and his brothers reconcile.

Jacob's family migrates to Egypt. 1876 BC

  ◆ Jacob blesses his sons before his death.

      ◆ Death of Joseph

Israel enslaved in Egypt. (dates unknown)

SONS OF JACOB (ISRAEL)

1. Reuben
2. Simeon
3. Levi
4. Judah
5. Dan
6. Naphtali
7. Gad
8. Asher
9. Issachar
10. Zebulun
11. Joseph
12. Benjamin

1800 BC	1700 BC	1600 BC

Israelites in Egypt 430 years

Joseph 110 years

LEVITICUS 📙　　📙 DEUTERONOMY

📙 EXODUS　　　　　📙 NUM.　📙 JOSHUA　📙 JUDGES

◆ Moses flees Egypt.

◆ God speaks to Moses from a burning bush.

◆ 10 plagues on Egypt

◆ First Passover

Birth of Moses ◆

Moses drawn out of the Nile. 1526 BC

Exodus
1446 BC
(high date)

Moses raised by ◆
Pharaoh's daughter.

◆ Parting of the Sea

◆ Songs of Moses and Miriam

◈ Mosaic covenant

◆ Tabernacle built.

◆ Ten Commandments given.

◆ Ark of the covenant constructed.

◆ Israelites spy out Canaan.

◆ Death of Moses

Joshua leads the conquest.
1406 BC

Some scholars date the exodus at a low date of 1290 BC, in which case the era of the judges would be shorter.
This time line follows a high date of 1446 BC.

◆ Rahab saves the spies.

◆ Walls of Jericho fall.

1600 BC	1500 BC	1400 BC	1300 BC

Wilderness
40 years

Israelites in Egypt 430 years

Conquest of Canaan
7 years

Moses 120 years

8

Egyptian Empire (New Kingdom)

📕 1 CHRONICLES

📕 1 SAMUEL   📕 2 SAMUEL

📕 RUTH   ◆ Samuel leads Israel.

◆ Ruth marries Boaz.   ◆ Israel demands a king.

👑 **Saul:** First king of Israel
1051 BC

◆ Exodus
1290 BC (low date)

◆ David is anointed by Samuel.

◆ David kills Goliath.

Judges of Israel
(dates unknown)

◆ Death of Saul and Jonathan.

👑 David becomes king.

◆ David brings the ark to Jerusalem.

◈ Davidic covenant

JUDGES

Othniel (40 years)
Ehud (80 years)
Shamgar (unknown)
Deborah (40 years)
Gideon (40 years)
Tola (23 years)
Jair (22 years)
Jephthah (6 years)
Ibzan (7 years)
Elon (10 years)
Abdon (8 years)
Samson (20 years)

◆ Eli the high priest   ◆ David's sin with Bathsheba

◆ Hannah dedicates her son, Samuel.

◆ Death of David

PSALMS 📕

PROVERBS 📕

1200 BC   1100 BC   1000 BC

Saul   David   Solomon

Era of the Judges 300 years

United Kingdom of Israel
120 years

2 CHRONICLES

1 KINGS   2 KINGS

King Jeroboam of Israel

King Rehoboam of Judah

JONAH

Jonah in the belly of a great fish

AMOS

King Jehoshaphat of Judah

HOSEA

King Ahab and Queen Jezebel of Israel

ISAIAH

MICAH

Elijah defeats the prophets of Baal.

Israel Falls to Assyria. 722 BC

Solomon becomes king.

Elijah taken to heaven.

Temple built in Jerusalem.

Elisha prophesies.

King Hezekiah restores the temple.

Death of Solomon

King Jehu of Israel

King Uzziah of Judah

Kingdom Divides. 931 BC

King Jeroboam II of Israel

SONG OF SONGS

ECCLESIASTES

Kings and rulers are shown by length of reign and prophets by length of prophetic ministry.

900 BC	800 BC	700 BC

Solomon

Isaiah 59 years

Northern Kingdom of Israel 209 years

Southern Kingdom of Judah 345 years

Assyrian Empire

EZRA | NEHEMIAH

📖 JEREMIAH 👑 King Cyrus of Persia

📖 HABAKKUK 📖 MALACHI

📖 LAMENTATIONS 📖 JOEL

📖 OBADIAH

👑 King Nebuchadnezzar of Babylon

📖 DANIEL 📖 HAGGAI

📖 EZEKIEL 📖 ZECHARIAH

◆ 1st Return: Zerubbabel

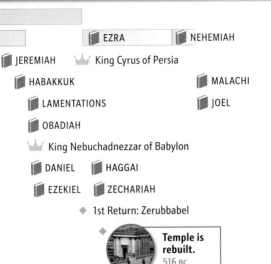

Temple is rebuilt.
516 BC

📖 NAHUM

📖 ZEPHANIAH 📖 ESTHER

👑 King Josiah finds the book of the law.

👑 Queen Esther

◆ Purim established.

Judah Falls to Babylon.
586 BC

◆ 2nd return: Ezra

◆ Ezra's reforms

◆ 3rd Return: Nehemiah

◆ Temple destroyed.

◆ Walls of Jerusalem rebuilt.

600 BC	500 BC	400 BC

Jeremiah 44 years

Daniel 70 years

Between the Old and New Testaments 400 years

Ezekiel 22 years

Exile 70 years

Babylonian Empire   Medo-Persian Empire   11

Alexander the Great conquers Judea. 332 BC

◆ Jewish self-rule begins; free from Seleucid control.

◆ Spartacus leads a slave revolt.

◆ Hellenization begins.

◆ Death of Alexander

Pompey conquers Jerusalem for Rome. 63 BC

◆ Alexander's empire splits.

◆ Ptolemy captures Jerusalem.

◆ First Triumvirate: Julius Caesar, Crassus, Pompey

◆ Earliest Dead Sea Scrolls written.

Herod the Great rules Judea.

◆ Septuagint: translation of Hebrew Scriptures into Greek

Herod begins ◆ expansion of temple complex.

◆ Seleucids defeat the Ptolemies.

BETWEEN THE TESTAMENTS

After the end of Old Testament history, the Persian Empire gave way to the Greeks, who brought their language, religion, and culture to conquered territories (Hellenization). Though Jews experienced a short period of independence, the Roman Empire came to rule the region through the time of Jesus and the early church.

◆ Antiochus IV Epiphanes desecrates the temple.

◆ Maccabean Revolt led by Judas Maccabeus.

Hanukkah: Temple rededicated. 164 BC

◆ Pharisees and Sadducees established as religious groups.

◆ Hasmonean dynasty

Events in the intertestamental period are not recorded in the 66 books of the Bible.

300 BC	200 BC	100 BC

Between the Old and New Testaments 400 years

Greek Empire

Herod the Great

Ptolemies   Seleucids

Hasmoneans

LUKE

 MATTHEW

◆ Annunciation: Mary will bear a son, Jesus, through the Holy Spirit.

◆ Birth of John the Baptist

◆ Joseph and Mary go to Bethlehem.

◆ **Birth of Christ** 4 BC

THE FOUR GOSPELS

The first four books of the New Testament narrate the ministry of Jesus the Messiah, with Luke and Matthew also describing events just before and after his birth. The gospels give us four viewpoints of Jesus' words and deeds. But together, they tell one story and one message that points to the cross and life beyond the grave.

◆ Infant Jesus is recognized at the temple as the Messiah.

◆ Magi from the east visit Jesus.

◆ Joseph, Mary, and Jesus flee to Egypt to escape Herod.

◆ Death of Herod

   ◆ Joseph, Mary, and Jesus settle in Nazareth.

◆ **Jesus** (age 12) amazes teachers at the temple. AD 8

AD 1	AD 10	AD 20

Caesar Augustus

Emperor Tiberius

Herod Antipas

Roman Empire

ACTS

MARK

JOHN

Holy Spirit at Pentecost
AD 30

◆ Peter and John preach the gospel in Jerusalem.

◆ Stephen martyred in Jerusalem.

Baptism of Jesus
AD 27

◆ Philip ministers in Judea and Samaria.

◆ Ethiopian official baptized.

◆ Paul's conversion on the road to Damascus

◆ Temptation of Jesus

◆ First miracle: water into wine

◆ Paul in Arabia, Jerusalem, and Tarsus

◆ Jesus gathers disciples, teaches, heals, performs miracles, and raises the dead.

◆ Peter takes the gospel to gentiles (Cornelius).

◆ Sermon on the Mount

◆ Death of John the Baptist

◆ Barnabas brings Paul to the church in Antioch.

◈ New covenant in Jesus

◆ Triumphal entry into Jerusalem

◆ James (apostle) martyred.

◆ Olivet Discourse

◆ Last Supper

◆ Peter's miraculous escape from prison

Death and Resurrection of Jesus AD 30

◆ Death of Herod Agrippa I

◆ Great Commission

◆ Jesus ascends to heaven.

AD 30	AD 40

Ministry of Jesus 3 years

Early travels

Emperor Tiberius

Emperor Caligula

Pontius Pilate

Herod Agrippa I

Herod Antipas

Roman Empire

1st Missionary Journey: Paul and Barnabas AD 47

◆ Paul under house arrest in Rome for 2 years.

📗 EPHESIANS

📗 HEBREWS

📗 PHILIPPIANS

📗 JUDE

📗 JAMES

📗 GALATIANS

📗 COLOSSIANS

📗 PHILEMON

📗 2 TIMOTHY

◆ Jerusalem Council

◆ 2nd Missionary Journey: Paul and Silas

◆ James (brother of Jesus) martyred.

📗 1 THESSALONIANS

📗 1 TIMOTHY

📗 2 THESSALONIANS

📗 TITUS

📗 1 PETER

◆ 3rd Missionary Journey: Paul, Timothy, and others

📗 2 PETER

📗 1 CORINTHIANS

◆ Nero's persecution of Christians begins.

📗 2 CORINTHIANS

◆ Paul and Peter imprisoned in Rome.

📗 ROMANS

◆ Paul in prison for 2 years

◆ Jewish uprising against Romans in Jerusalem

◆ Paul stands trial.

Paul shipwrecked on Malta. ◆

Paul and Peter martyred in Rome. AD 66–68

◆

AD 50	AD 60	AD 70

Paul's Journeys

1st 2nd   3rd   Prison   Rome   Later travels and prison

Emperor Claudius   Emperor Nero

Herod Agrippa II

1 JOHN

2 JOHN

3 JOHN

Temple destroyed by Romans.
AD 70

◆ Masada falls to the Romans.

  ◆ Josephus writes *Jewish War*.

    ◆ Mt. Vesuvius erupts.

      ◆ The *Didache* (early Christian practices) written.

Colosseum in Rome completed.
AD 80

    ◆ Emperor Domitian declares himself "Lord and God."

    ◆ Domitian persecutes Christians.

AD 70	AD 80	AD 90

Emperor Titus

Emperor Vespasian   Emperor Domitian

Herod Agrippa II

Roman Empire

◆ Josephus writes *Antiquities of the Jews*.

◆ **John** is exiled on Patmos.

📕 REVELATION

    ◆ Clement, bishop of Rome

      ◆ Rise of Gnostic heresies within the church

        ◆ Death of John in Ephesus

        ◆ Writings of early church leaders: Clement, Ignatius, Polycarp

        ◆ Churches established as far as Carthage, Edessa, Alexandria, and Rome.

Most events after Acts are not recorded in the Bible.

AD 100	AD 110

Emperor
Nerva
        Emperor Trajan

BEGINNINGS

CREATION
Genesis 1–2

> "In the beginning
> God created
> the heavens
> and the earth."
>
> GENESIS 1:1

The first chapter of Genesis tells how God brought form to the formless and filled the emptiness with life. "Now the earth was formless and empty ... and God said, 'Let there be light, and there was light'" (Gen. 1:2–3). With the power of his word, God created light where there was none, put the galaxies in space, made birds to fill the air and fish to fill the seas, and like a potter at his wheel, he formed the first human being from the dust of the ground. What an extraordinary sight that must have been!

The creation story reveals who God is. He is the Creator who gives life to humanity and all living things. In this story, we see God as designer, artist, architect, and life-giver; a good and loving God who takes delight in his creation.

A FALLEN WORLD
Genesis 3–11

The first two chapters of Genesis portray a picture of the world that is "very good" (Gen. 1:31). God put the first man and woman in the garden of Eden, a place where they cared for God's creation and God cared for them. Both Adam and Eve were naked and felt no shame (Gen. 2:25).

Consider the world as it is today. It's easy to see that many things are not the way they should be. If everything was once so good, how did it go so wrong? The next chapter in Genesis answers this question. As image bearers of God, Adam and Eve had a choice: trust in the goodness of their creator or go their own way, rebelling against the kind of life God had given them. God issued them one restriction: "You must not eat from the tree of the knowledge of good and evil, for when you eat from it you will certainly die" (Gen. 2:17).

Deceived by a manipulative serpent, Eve chose the fruit of the one tree that was off limits. (Revelation 12:9 and 20:2 point to the involvement of Satan—"that ancient serpent"—in this deception in the garden.) Adam also ate the fruit and things were never the same. Shame, followed by hiding from God, was their immediate response (Gen. 3:7–8). The man and woman had known only the goodness of God. In rebellion against their maker, they came to know evil as well.

The following stories in the book of Genesis give a clear—and at times disturbing—portrait of the effects of sin in the world. This is especially seen in the story of Adam and Eve's sons, where Cain, jealous that Abel's sacrifice was accepted by God when his was not, murders his own brother. It's seen in the account of the rampant wickedness in the days of Noah and God's judgment upon the earth in the form of a massive flood in which only Noah and his family were saved from destruction. Later, it's seen when God confuses the languages and scatters a people who tried to build a name for themselves with the tower of Babel.

GENESIS

The book of Genesis covers from the creation of the world to the story of Joseph in Egypt around 1800 BC. The stories take place in Mesopotamia, Canaan, and Egypt. Genesis is a book about beginnings. The word *genesis* comes from a Greek word meaning "to be born." Chapters 1–3 explain the origin of the world and humanity, followed by the origin of nations in chapters 4–11; and chapters 12–50 deal with the origin of Israel.

THE PATRIARCHS

ABRAHAM AND SARAH
Genesis 12–24

Starting in Genesis 12, we see God forging a path of redemption through one special—though far from perfect—family. God called Abraham and his family to migrate from Harran in Mesopotamia to the land of Canaan. God assured Abraham with a covenant—like a promise or pledge—

> "The LORD said to Abram, 'Go from your country, your people and your father's household to the land I will show you.'"
>
> GENESIS 12:1

that God would bless him and his family. Throughout Abraham's story in Genesis, God reaffirms this covenant with Abraham on seven different occasions. The covenant included these promises: Abraham and his wife Sarah would have a son (Gen. 18:1–15); all nations would be blessed through Abraham's descendants (Gen. 12:1–3); the land that God would show Abraham would belong to his descendants (Gen. 12:7; 22:15–18); and Abraham's descendants would be as numerous as the stars in the sky and the sand on the seashore (Gen. 13:14–17;15:1–21; 17:1–21; 22:17).

But there was a problem—at least from a human point of view. Abraham and Sarah were old and childless. How could they have a multitude of descendants, let alone even one descendant? God was promising them the impossible. In the ancient world, infertility was considered cause for a husband to divorce his wife or to have heirs through concubines or slaves. Rather than continue to wait for God's promise to be fulfilled, Abraham, at Sarah's urging, had a son named Ishmael with Sarah's slave, Hagar. Despite their attempt to shortcut God's promises, God kept his covenant, and Sarah, well-advanced in age, bore a son, Isaac. God was faithful to the covenant, but it was according to his timetable, not theirs. In fact, Isaac was born a full twenty-five years after God had first made the covenant with Abraham (Gen. 12:4; 21:5).

As we learn from the rest of the Bible, God's plan was even bigger than what Abraham and Sarah may have understood. Not only would their descendants be numerous, but the Messiah, Jesus the Savior, would be born through Abraham's lineage. Remember that Genesis is a book of beginnings; it tells not only the beginning of the nation of Israel through a son promised to Abraham and Sarah, but it also explains the beginning of a history which would ultimately lead to Christ Jesus, the Son of God.

JACOB'S FAMILY
Genesis 25–36

After Abraham's and Sarah's deaths, the biblical narrative turns to Isaac's twin sons, Jacob and Esau, but particularly Jacob. At birth, Jacob was given his name, translated as "he grasps at the heel," an ancient Hebrew expression that meant "he deceives" (Gen. 25:26). Later in Jacob's life, God changed his name to Israel which means "struggles with God" (Gen. 32:28). Both names suggest a man (and also a family) in a tug-of-war with God and each other.

The stories in this section of Genesis detail how God's chosen family struggled. They struggled with God—Jacob did so, literally in Genesis 32. They struggled with each other—deceiving, fearing, and betraying. For example, Jacob and his mother Rebekah tricked an aged and blind Isaac into giving Jacob the blessing that belonged to Esau (Gen. 27:1–45). Jacob fled when Esau vowed revenge. It would be twenty years before the brothers would meet again. Jacob was fooled by Laban, who tricked him into marrying Leah when Jacob had wanted to marry Rachel. The deceiver had become the deceived. In the end, Jacob married both sisters (Gen. 29:15–30). (Having multiple wives was a common practice in the ancient world.) Leah and Rachel competed for their husband's affection by having as many children for him as possible—twelve sons and one daughter in total.

There were, however, times when this family turned toward God, and God turned toward them. Jacob received an amazing glimpse into the heavenly realm, a dream of a stairway to heaven. The Lord reassured Jacob that the promises made to his grandfather Abraham would be fulfilled. An awestruck Jacob declared, "How awesome is this place! ... The LORD will be my God" (Gen. 28:10–22). After twenty years of estrangement from his brother Esau, Jacob returned to Canaan and encountered Esau. Fearing for his life, Jacob humbled himself and prayed to God for protection. Much to Jacob's surprise, Esau did not take revenge, but instead embraced and forgave Jacob (Gen. 32:1–33:4). The Lord chose to work his will through this family's broken lives, rescuing them from certain doom when their lies and foolishness got them in trouble.

JOSEPH IN EGYPT
Genesis 37–50

Against the backdrop of this very flawed family, the story of Joseph stands out. The book of Genesis devotes thirteen chapters (that's about one fourth of the book) to Joseph, the eleventh son of Jacob. His story provides us with an example of a young man from an unstable family who chose to rely on God when so much of his future seemed hopeless.

Joseph's older brothers resented him. In fact, they were so jealous of him that they sold him to slave traders and told their father that Joseph had been killed by a wild animal. As a slave in Egypt, Joseph had no connections, no money, no status, and no protection from harm. But he did have one person on his side: "The Lord was with Joseph" (Gen. 39:2, 3, 21, 23). That made all the difference. Joseph didn't just survive in this foreign land, he thrived. Though he faced hardship and injustices, Joseph eventually became a top official in Egypt. The Lord was indeed with Joseph.

When his brothers traveled to Egypt to buy food during a famine, Joseph was faced with a choice: forgiveness or revenge. He chose forgiveness. He understood that God had a bigger plan that would succeed in spite of human sinfulness. He declared to his brothers, "You intended to harm me, but God intended it for good to accomplish what is now being done, the saving of many lives" (Gen. 50:20).

This part of the biblical story—and the book of Genesis—ends with God's chosen family living in Egypt. Jacob and his family had migrated to Egypt to escape the famine. Though they grew in number, as God's covenant said they would, they were far from the land God had promised.

JOB

The book of Job tells the story of an upright man whose life is overthrown and eventually restored. Job's story may have occurred during the era of Abraham, Isaac, and Jacob in an unknown location simply called "the land of Uz," possibly Edom (Job 1:1). The book is written in a style of ancient Hebrew known as wisdom literature. Rather than dealing directly with Israel's history, wisdom literature—like Job, Proverbs, and Ecclesiastes—reflects on universal themes that are relevant for all people in all places.

MOSES

Exodus 1–18

> *"I am the LORD your God, who brought you out of Egypt, out of the land of slavery. You shall have no other gods before me."*
>
> EXODUS 20:2

The book of Exodus opens with the descendants of Jacob (called Hebrews or Israelites) growing numerous in the land of Egypt for many years. God had blessed them, but the Egyptian rulers saw their success as a threat and enslaved them (Ex. 1:8–11). Their masters "worked them ruthlessly" (Ex. 1:13). Even worse, to prevent further population growth, Pharaoh ordered every Hebrew newborn boy to be thrown into the Nile River! It was during this time that a Hebrew baby named Moses was born. Moses was miraculously saved from death in the Nile and raised by Pharaoh's daughter. He grew up as a member of Pharaoh's household, but God had chosen Moses for something much greater than the royal Egyptian court.

As an adult, Moses's life took an unexpected turn when he was forced to flee Egypt as a fugitive. He settled in the distant land of Midian as a shepherd, ready to live the rest of his life in obscurity. But one day, while Moses was tending flocks, God called to him from a burning bush: "Moses! Moses!" (Ex. 3:4). Moses's divine directive was to go back to Egypt and confront Pharaoh to let God's people leave Egypt.

Though Moses initially balked at the enormity of the task, he obeyed God and went back to Egypt and confronted Pharaoh, the ruler of the most powerful kingdom the ancient world had known. The Egyptians considered Pharaoh to be a god who was responsible for maintaining cosmic order. Moses's initial hesitancy to challenge Pharaoh makes sense. Moses was confronting an Egyptian deity! On the surface, Moses was facing off against Pharaoh and his magicians; yet it was really the God of Moses facing the false gods of the Egyptians. After God sent ten terrible plagues upon Egypt—the tenth of which took the life of Pharaoh's own son—Pharaoh relented to Moses's demands and let God's people leave.

In their exodus journey from Egypt, God continued to demonstrate his goodness and might by providing for and protecting his people. When the Egyptian army pursued them, God parted the sea for the Israelites to pass through on dry ground and destroyed Pharaoh's army with walls of water crashing in on them (Ex. 14:1–31). He provided manna and quail for food in the desert, just enough for each day (Ex. 16:13–18). After three months of traveling, God led the Israelites to the base of Mount Sinai.

AT MOUNT SINAI
Exodus 19–40; Leviticus 1–27; Numbers 1–9

Moses and the Israelites spent about two years camped at the foot of Mount Sinai. What happens within this short period of time accounts for fifty-eight chapters of the Old Testament! Many of these chapters—including the entire book of Leviticus—consist of the instructions God gave his people about how to live as a "kingdom of priests and a holy nation" (Ex. 19:6).

At Sinai, God called Moses up to the mountain to meet with him. Moses became the mediator of a covenant between God and Israel. Through Moses, God gave the Ten Commandments (Ex. 20:2–17); detailed instructions for building the tabernacle and its furnishings, including the most sacred item, the ark of the covenant (Ex. 25:8, 22); and laws to govern the people's lives, worship practices, priesthood, and society.

THE WILDERNESS WANDERINGS
Numbers 10–36; Deuteronomy 1–34

After two years in the desert of Sinai, at the Lord's command, Moses and the Israelites set out toward the promised land of Canaan (Num. 10:11–13). Moses sent twelve spies into Canaan to explore the land. When the spies returned, ten advised the Israelites not to go in because it was too dangerous and the inhabitants too fierce. Only two, Caleb and Joshua, urged the people to trust God and enter the land. But the people listened to the ten instead: "All the Israelites grumbled against Moses and Aaron, and the whole assembly said to them, 'If only we had died in Egypt! Or in this wilderness!'" (Num. 14:2). Though God didn't send them back to Egypt, he did give them their second request: to die in the wilderness. The Lord declared to Moses that this faithless generation would not enter the promised land (Num. 14:20–35). The Israelites lived as nomads in the wilderness for forty years (counting from the year they left Egypt).

At the end of the wilderness wanderings, the adults who emerged from Egypt in the exodus had died; their children, now grown, stood at the edge of the promised land in the plains of Moab. The book of Deuteronomy consists of Moses's speeches on these plains to this next generation. Though God did not allow Moses to enter the promised land, he gave Moses a view of the land from Mount Nebo before Moses's death (Deut. 43).

EXODUS

The book of Exodus (which means "going out") begins about three hundred years after Joseph's story. The book tells how God, through Moses, led the descendants of Jacob (Israel) out of slavery in Egypt to Mount Sinai. The book closes with the Israelites at Sinai where God's glory fills the tabernacle, a sign of God's presence.

LEVITICUS

The book of Leviticus takes place within the two years that the Israelites spent camped at the foot of Mount Sinai. Leviticus is a series of divine directives about sacrifices, priestly duties, ritual purity, feasts of Israel, and holy ("set apart") living. Though the book's name is derived from the Greek word *leyiticon* which means "things concerning the Levites," the instructions were for the entire nation of Israel.

NUMBERS

The book of Numbers narrates the years of wilderness
wanderings after the Israelites left Mount Sinai. It's named
Numbers because of the two censuses recorded in chapters
1 and 26. In Exodus, God had promised the Israelites that he
would be with them on their way out of captivity. In Numbers,
we see God remaining faithful to this promise despite his
people's rebellion. The book ends with the Israelites camped in
Moab just outside the promised land.

DEUTERONOMY

The book of Deuteronomy takes place about forty years
after the exodus on the plains of Moab at the edge of the
promised land. The book's name comes from the Greek word
deuteronomion meaning "second law." Deuteronomy consists
of encouraging and challenging speeches Moses gave to the
next generation as they were about to enter Canaan. The book
closes with Moses viewing the promised land from Mount
Nebo just before his death.

THE PROMISED LAND

CONQUEST OF CANAAN
Joshua 1–24

Joshua was Moses's appointed successor to lead the Israelites into Canaan (Num. 27:18–20). Joshua had been one of the two spies who returned from the promised land with a favorable report for Moses. Like Moses, Joshua had a promise from God: "I will never leave you nor forsake you" (Josh. 1:5).

> *"Be strong and courageous. Do not be afraid; do not be discouraged, for the LORD your God will be with you wherever you go."*
>
> JOSHUA 1:9

The entry into the land began with a miraculous sign of God's presence. God parted the Jordan River so the people entered across dry land. This was reminiscent of the Red Sea parting as Moses and the Israelites left Egypt. The conquest of cities in Canaan began with God tumbling the massive walls of Jericho. Rahab, a Canaanite woman in Jericho who wisely understood what was happening, said, "I know that the LORD has given you this land.... For the LORD your God is God in heaven above and earth below" (Josh. 2:9, 11). When Jericho fell, she and her family were spared because of her faith and assistance to Israel.

Then, Joshua and his army moved through the land conquering cities. In all the battles, God was their behind-the-scenes military commander, present and empowering

(Josh. 5:13–15). Feared by the people of the land, the Israelites quickly settled throughout Canaan and Joshua allotted specific territories to the different tribes of Israel. The book of Joshua closes with Joshua's farewell address in which he reminds the people to remain faithful to God as God was faithful to them. Joshua memorably declared, "Choose for yourselves this day whom you will serve, whether the gods your ancestors served beyond the Euphrates, or the gods of the Amorites, in whose land you are living. But as for me and my household, we will serve the LORD" (Josh. 24:15). Joshua died at 110 years old and was buried in the promised land.

JOSHUA

The book of Joshua covers the years after Moses's death when Joshua led the Israelites into the promised land. The conquest of Canaan is estimated to have taken about seven years. Chapters 1–12 cover Joshua's conquest of Canaan, and chapters 13–22 explain the allotment of the land among the tribes of Israel. Chapters 23–24 are Joshua's farewell.

THE JUDGES
Judges 1–21

Joshua's death left the tribes of Israel without a central leader. The Lord was supposed to be their King, but as we read at the beginning of the book of Judges, "Another generation grew up who knew neither the LORD nor what he had done for Israel" (Judg. 2:10). Moses had told the people, "Remember the LORD your God," but this new generation soon forgot (Deut. 8:18). The awesome victories of the past became distant, forgotten tales. The book of Judges portrays repeated cycles of sin and deliverance during this era:

Sin: Though the Israelites had conquered many key cities in Canaan, they settled alongside the remaining Canaanites in the land (Judg. 2:20–23). They often turned to the false gods of the Canaanites instead of trusting in the one true God to provide for their needs.

Oppression: In response to Israel's sins, God allowed other nations to oppress Israel. This oppression wasn't a mere inconvenience; in the ancient world, it was brutal and violent.

Repentance: In desperation, the Israelites eventually cried out to God: "We have sinned against you, forsaking our God and serving the Baals" (Judg. 10:10).

Deliverance: In his mercy, God raised up a leader (a "judge") to deliver Israel from their oppressors. Notable among the twelve judges in the book of Judges are Deborah, Gideon, and Samson.

Peace: With the success of each judge, Israel experienced a time of peace. But eventually Israel fell back into worshiping other gods, and the cycle would start again.

JUDGES

The book of Judges takes place in Canaan during the era between Joshua and Samuel. The first two chapters of Judges explain how the conquest of Canaan was incomplete. Chapters 3–16 tell the stories of twelve judges of Israel. The final chapters, 17–21, describe a time of sin and strife among the tribes of Israel.

RUTH

The book of Ruth takes place in Bethlehem (and for a short time in Moab) during the latter part of the era of the judges, a time when Israel's spiritual and social life was a mess (Ruth 1:1). The story is about Naomi, a widow who had lost all hope; her daughter-in-law Ruth, a faithful foreigner; Boaz, a compassionate guardian-redeemer; but mostly, it's about the God who restored their lives with joy. God's love shines through this story in the lives of ordinary people who showed extraordinary kindness and loyalty during a time when those qualities were hard to find.

THE UNITED KINGDOM

SAMUEL, SAUL, AND DAVID
1 Samuel 1–31; 1 Chronicles 1–10

Samuel led Israel both as a prophet
and the last judge of the era of
judges. Late in his life, the Israelites
made it clear that they didn't want
another judge to succeed him.
They demanded a king like other
nations. God explained to Samuel,
"It is not you they have rejected,
but they have rejected me as their
king" (1 Sam. 8:7). Though God
warned the Israelites that having a
king would come with many unpleasant strings attached,
the people insisted. So God instructed Samuel to anoint a
man named Saul as Israel's first king.

> "If my people, who
> are called by my
> name, will humble
> themselves and
> pray and seek my
> face and turn from
> their wicked ways,
> then I will hear
> from heaven, and
> I will forgive their
> sin and will heal
> their land."
>
> 2 CHRONICLES 7:14

Saul was handsome, young, and tall. He looked the part
of a king. Though Saul had initial success as king, in time,
he disobeyed the word of the Lord and ignored God's
instructions. This prompted Samuel to declare a fateful
prophecy: "Your kingdom will not endure; the LORD
has sought out a man after his own heart" (1 Sam. 13:14).
Another king would be chosen.

David was the youngest of eight brothers, a teenager who
was given the chore of tending sheep. When God sent

Samuel to David's family in Bethlehem, Samuel thought that surely the eldest brother—the tall one—would be Israel's next king. But as it turned out, God had chosen the youngest son, David the shepherd. (The Hebrew word for *youngest* in 1 Samuel 16:11 also means *smallest*.) "The LORD does not look at the things people look at. People look at the outward appearance, but the LORD looks at the heart" (1 Sam. 16:7). God had called David to leave the pastures of sheep to go shepherd the people of Israel.

Once anointed by Samuel, David quickly rose to prominence in Israel. He defeated a giant Philistine warrior Goliath with a simple slingshot. He forged an unbreakable friendship with Saul's son Jonathan, the heir apparent. He even married the king's daughter, Michal. But then it all came tumbling down. In jealousy and rage, Saul nearly killed David, so David fled Jerusalem.

For fourteen years, David moved throughout the wilderness of Judah, living as a fugitive from Saul. During this time, David built up a militia six hundred men strong (1 Sam. 27:2). He raided towns and even lived for a time with the Philistines—the enemy of Israel! The shepherd boy had become a man of war. Years later, this would be cited as a reason God prevented David from building the temple (1 Chron. 22:8).

Saul and his sons, including Jonathan, died in a battle against the Philistines. This put David in a position to take hold of the kingship for which God had anointed him years before. David sought the Lord, asking, "Where shall I go?" "To Hebron," the Lord answered (2 Sam. 2:1). And David, a man after God's own heart, listened and obeyed.

KING DAVID
2 Samuel 1–24; 1 Chronicles 11–29; 1 Kings 1–2

In Hebron, David was made king over Judah and he ruled from there seven and a half years. Then the rest of the tribes made David king over all of Israel. David's first act as king of Israel was to make Jerusalem the national capital and bring the ark of the covenant into the city—a sign of God's power and presence.

When the ark entered Jerusalem to the sound of trumpets and cheering, David was "dancing before the Lord with all his might" in celebratory abandon (2 Sam. 6:14). Almost half of the 150 psalms in the book of Psalms are attributed to David. These psalms reveal a man unhindered in expressing his heart's joyful praise for God's goodness, but also his deep sorrow in times of suffering.

God made a covenant with David: "Your kingdom will endure forever.... Your throne will be established forever" (2 Sam. 7:16). David brought national unity that Saul was not able to achieve between the warring tribes.

But at the height of his success, the king sinned gravely. David took for himself Bathsheba, the wife of Uriah, one of his elite military leaders, and then he had Uriah killed on the battlefield. Though David repented and received forgiveness from God, the consequences of his sin affected his family and kingdom (2 Sam. 11–12). David's story in the book of 2 Samuel from this point on is a series of troubles. One of his sons assaulted his daughter (chapter 13). Another son, Absalom, attempted to usurp the throne and declare himself king (chapter 15). Disloyal leaders in David's kingdom attempted yet another coup (chapter 20). War between Israel and the Philistines resumed (chapter 21). A plague caused thousands in Israel to die (chapter 24).

David ruled Israel for forty years. Some of his last words were to his son Solomon who inherited the throne. Spoken from years of personal experience, David told his son, "Serve [the Lord] with wholehearted devotion and with a willing mind, for the Lord searches every heart and understands every desire and every thought" (1 Chron. 28:9).

KING SOLOMON
2 Chronicles 1–9; 1 Kings 3–11

King Solomon reigned during the golden age of Israel, a time of national and economic prosperity. Solomon began his kingship by asking God for one thing: wisdom. He desired to govern God's people with "a discerning heart" (1 Kings 3:9). "God gave Solomon wisdom and very great insight, and a breadth of understanding as measureless as the sand on the seashores" (1 Kings 4:29). During Solomon's reign, he expanded the boundaries of Israel, achieved economic successes, constructed a magnificent palace, built the first temple in Jerusalem, and placed the ark of the covenant in the most holy room of the temple.

Solomon's wisdom is recorded in the books of Proverbs, Ecclesiastes, Song of Songs, and even two psalms (72, 127). First Kings 4:32 says that by the end of his life, Solomon had spoken over 3,000 proverbs and written 1,005 songs!

But King Solomon eventually married over 700 foreign wives and had 300 concubines! Royal marriages like this in the ancient world were a way of forming political and economic alliances between nations. Solomon may have seen his many marriages as a means to strengthen his kingdom, but in the end, this proved to be a foolish path to follow. In his old age, Solomon set up numerous places of worship for the gods of his many wives, and no longer was his heart "fully devoted to the LORD his God" (1 Kings 11:4).

During most of Solomon's reign, Israel was united and prosperous. Upon his death, however, Solomon left behind a fragile kingdom on the verge of breaking apart.

1 AND 2 SAMUEL

The books of Samuel cover from the latter part of the era of the judges through David's reign and take place primarily in Judah. Some sections of the books may have been written by Samuel, Nathan, and Gad (see 1 Chron. 29:29–30). These books illustrate God's blessing upon the faithful, the disastrous consequences of sin.

1 AND 2 KINGS

The books of Kings cover the time period from King Solomon's reign through the division and slow collapse of Israel and Judah. The author is unknown, but Jewish tradition attributes the books to the prophet Jeremiah. These books explain how the kingdoms of Israel and Judah were conquered and their people exiled because of their sins. The books also include the stories of the prophets Elijah and Elisha.

1 AND 2 CHRONICLES

Both books of Chronicles were written after the exile, around 450–400 BC, by an unknown author. Jewish tradition attributes the books to Ezra. The books cover a long period of history, from the death of King Saul to the fall of Judah and the exile. These books were written to encourage the exiles who returned to Judah by connecting them to their history.

PSALMS

The psalms were compiled from as early as the time of David, around 1000 BC, to as late as Ezra, around 450 BC. Psalms is a collection of 150 Hebrew songs, prayers, and poems. At least 73 psalms are attributed to David and two to Solomon.

PROVERBS

Proverbs was compiled over a time span of about 900–700 BC. The book is a collection of memorable sayings that help people live wise and godly lives. Most of the book was written by Solomon (Prov. 1:1; 10:1; 25:1), but other authors also contributed (Prov. 22:17; 24:23; 30:1; 31:1).

ECCLESIASTES

Ecclesiastes (which means "the teacher") is anonymous, but tradition holds that Solomon authored this philosophical book late in life. He ponders the meaning—or meaninglessness ("vanity")—of the things of life: work, wealth, pleasures, wisdom, and death. He concludes by saying, "Fear God and keep his commandments, for this is the duty of all mankind" (Eccl. 12:13).

SONG OF SONGS (SONG OF SOLOMON)

Though Solomon is identified as the author in the first verse, some parts of the book appear to be written by others and were composed at a later date. This book is a love song that moves from courtship, the wedding ceremony, and through the banquet celebration. Solomon himself had hundreds of wives (hardly an example of marital faithfulness!); rather than a description from Solomon's own life, the song can be seen as an expression of an ideal experience within a loving, covenant relationship.

THE DIVIDED KINGDOM

KINGS AND PROPHETS
1 Kings 12–22; 2 Kings 1–25; 2 Chronicles 10–36

> "Before me no god was formed, nor will there be one after me. I, even I, am the LORD, and apart from me there is no savior."
>
> ISAIAH 43:10–11

After King Solomon's death, old tribal loyalties rumbling below the surface appeared again. Civil war broke out between the ten northern tribes and the two southern tribes. In the south, King Solomon's son, Rehoboam, claimed kingship over the region of Judah. This territory became known as the Southern Kingdom of Judah. Under Rehoboam's rule, "the people engaged in all the detestable practices of the nations the LORD had driven out before the Israelites" (1 Kings 14:24). In the north, Jeroboam, a former official in Solomon's court, was made ruler of the Northern Kingdom of Israel. With God's temple and the ark of the covenant in Jerusalem in the south, Jeroboam decided to give his people in the north new places of worship and new gods (1 Kings 12:28).

These two wicked kings, Rehoboam and Jeroboam, were the first in a series of rulers—nineteen in Israel and twenty in Judah—most of whom did evil in the eyes of the Lord. God sent prophets to his rebellious people with words of warning. We read in the book of Amos about the prophet's warnings to an apathetic people who had turned their backs on God and exploited the poor and vulnerable.

Despite military threats from powerful kingdoms like Assyria and Egypt, this was still a time of economic prosperity for Israel. And who would listen to prophets preaching doom when everything seemed to be okay? To keep Assyria and Egypt at bay, the kings of both Israel and Judah formed political alliances with these nations and adopted their gods and worship practices. The prophet Isaiah spoke out strongly against these alliances, but as was often the case, the kings didn't heed the prophet's warnings.

Notable for their wickedness were King Ahab of Israel and his wife Queen Jezebel (1 Kings 16:33). When the prophet Elijah defeated the priests of Baal on Mount Carmel, Jezebel vowed to kill him. God intervened and provided for Elijah, and in the end, God took Elijah up into heaven with a whirlwind, leaving the prophet Elisha to succeed him (2 Kings 2:11–12). Jezebel and Ahab, however, both met violent deaths of their own (1 Kings 22:29–38; 2 Kings 9:30–37).

Despite the wickedness in the land, there were moments of spiritual revival. King Hezekiah of Judah "did what was right in the eyes of the LORD" (2 Chron. 29:2). Hezekiah's reign was almost 250 years after King Solomon had built the temple. By Hezekiah's time, the people had abandoned God's temple. Hezekiah "opened the doors of the temple" and reinstituted worship, sacrifices, and the Passover celebration commemorating the exodus (2 Chron. 29:3). Revival broke out and the people smashed their idols and tore down the altars to other gods. But their devotion to the God of Israel didn't last long.

The Kingdom of Israel fell to Assyria in 722 BC and the Kingdom of Judah fell to Babylon in 586 BC. (Second Chronicles 36:15–16 and 2 Kings 17:13–18 explain why.)

The prophet Jeremiah lived to see the fall of Judah. God delivered a message through Jeremiah for those who had been taken into exile, who had suffered under the cruelty of Assyria and Babylon—and this message was one of hope: "When seventy years are completed for Babylon, I will come to you and fulfill my good promise to bring you back to this place. For I know the plans I have for you... plans to prosper you and not to harm you, plans to give you hope and a future" (Jer. 29:10–11).

ISAIAH

Isaiah, whose name means "the Lord saves," prophesied during the reign of four kings of Judah: Uzziah, Jotham, Ahaz and Hezekiah (Isa. 1:1). His ministry lasted more than fifty years, around 740–681 BC. He is also mentioned in 2 Kings 19–20, a story which parallels Isaiah 36–38. He was married to a prophetess and had at least two sons (Isa. 7:3; 8:3). Isaiah opposed Judah's alliances with pagan nations and urged the people to repent of their sins and put their hope in the coming Messiah (Isa. 9, 53).

JONAH

Jonah, whose name means "dove," lived during the reign of Jeroboam II of Israel (793–746 BC), so the story in the book of Jonah is believed to have taken place around that time, but an exact date is uncertain. God called the reluctant prophet to go to Nineveh, the capital of Assyria, Israel's enemy. After spending three days and nights in the belly of a great fish, the prophet obeyed God. When the Ninevites received God's mercy instead of wrath, Jonah became angry.

NAHUM

Nahum, whose name means "the Lord comforts," prophesied about a coming judgment upon Nineveh, the capital of Assyria, around 663–612 BC. When Assyria defeated Israel in 722 BC, the people of Judah watched as the Assyrians tortured and deported the Israelites. Nahum's words were meant to warn the Assyrians to repent, but also to assure Judah that Assyria's sins would not go unanswered by God. Assyria fell to Babylon in 612 BC.

AMOS

Amos, whose name means "burden bearer," prophesied to the Northern Kingdom of Israel, around 760–753 BC, some thirty years before it fell to Assyria. Amos was a shepherd and fig farmer called by God to prophesy against a materially prosperous Israel for treating the poor with injustice and betraying their covenant with God.

JEREMIAH

Jeremiah prophesied to the people of Judah around the time of Judah's oppression and fall to Babylon (626–582 BC). Sometimes called "the weeping prophet," Jeremiah pleaded with Judah to repent of their idolatry and arrogance. The people did not heed Jeremiah's message and he lived to see the fall of Judah to Babylon in 586 BC.

OBADIAH

Obadiah prophesied about Edom, Israel's neighboring nation, just after Judah fell to Babylon in 586 BC. The prophet pronounced judgment upon the people of Edom for their disregard and mistreatment of Judah. Eventually, Edom also fell to Babylon (Jer. 27:3–6).

LAMENTATIONS

The book of Lamentations dates to just after the fall of Judah to Babylon in 586 BC. Lamentations is a series of five grief poems (laments) over the destruction of Jerusalem and the temple. Although the book is anonymous, most traditions attribute it to Jeremiah (see 2 Chronicles 35:25).

ZEPHANIAH

Zephaniah, whose name means "the Lord has hidden," prophesied to the people of Judah during the reign of King

Josiah of Judah, around 641–628 BC. The prophet warned about the judgment coming on the day of the Lord. However, God promised that, in time, he would "gather the exiles" and "bring you home" (Zeph. 3:19–20).

HOSEA

Hosea, whose name means "salvation," prophesied to the Northern Kingdom of Israel during a time of decline and eventual fall to Assyria, around 752–722 BC. God instructed him to marry an unfaithful woman, Gomer, to serve as a real-life illustration of Israel's unfaithfulness and God's unfailing love for his people.

HABAKKUK

Habakkuk, whose name might come from the Hebrew word for "embrace," prophesied during a time of Babylonian oppression (609–598 BC), not long before Judah's demise at the hands of the Babylonians in 586 BC. In his book, he talks with God in a series of complaints and answers, grappling with how God's anger and justice relate to God's love and mercy.

MICAH

Micah, whose name means "who is like the Lord," prophesied to Israel and Judah during the time of Israel's decline and fall to Assyria, around 738–698 BC. Micah spoke against the leaders of Israel and Judah for their injustice, greed, and pride.

DANIEL IN BABYLON
Daniel 1–12

> "The God of heaven will set up a kingdom that will never be destroyed."
>
> DANIEL 2:44

Daniel was only a teenager when he was taken captive by the invading Babylonian army around 605 BC. He was deported from his homeland in Jerusalem and taken into service in the capital city of Babylon. Daniel, however, was determined not to live according to the standards of that world, but to God's standards.

The stories in the book of Daniel paint a portrait of a man fully committed to living a holy life in the midst of a pagan land, unashamed of his God. When Daniel correctly interpreted King Nebuchadnezzar's dream of a statue, he gave God the glory instead of taking credit himself: "No wise man, enchanter, magician or diviner can explain to the king the mystery he has asked about, but there is a God in heaven who reveals mysteries" (Dan. 2:27–28). In Daniel's later years, he continued to pray publicly three times a day, even when the king prohibited it. This landed Daniel in a den of lions. But God was there with Daniel and he shut the mouths of the lions, saving Daniel from certain death (Dan. 6).

DANIEL

Daniel lived most of his life in Babylon, around 605–535 BC, during the reigns of kings Nebuchadnezzar and Belshazzar of Babylon and Cyrus of Persia (Dan. 1:1; 5:1; 10:1). Daniel's name means "God is my judge." Chapters 1–6 recount stories of Daniel's and his friends' lives in exile. Chapters 7–12 contain Daniel's prophetic visions concerning the future, like the four great beasts from the sea and a "son of man" coming in the clouds of heaven (Dan. 7).

EZEKIEL IN EXILE
Ezekiel 1–48

While Daniel was navigating the royal court in Babylon, a priest named Ezekiel was living among the exiles in a Jewish settlement near Babylon. Ezekiel was taken captive from Judah to Babylonia about eight years after Daniel was taken. We know much less about Ezekiel's life than Daniel's, only that Ezekiel was married and at some point his wife died (Ezek. 24:18). Ezekiel was called by God to be a prophet, a "watchman" (Ezek. 3:17; 33:7).

The book of Ezekiel consists of judgment prophecies, laments, and visions of Israel's future restoration. The first thirty-two chapters show the prophet delivering God's warning of coming suffering to Judah and other nations. Ezekiel tried to get the message across to the people in any way possible. He employed unusual imagery, even acting out the coming destruction of Jerusalem by shaving his head and baking bread over a fire fueled by cow dung (Ezek. 4:15; 5:1). Judah would experience a time of suffering because God was judging them for their idolatry, murders, sexual sins, exploitation of the vulnerable, and alliances with pagan nations (Ezek. 22:1–12). Ezekiel's message from God was surely a difficult one to deliver!

The remainder of the book (chapters 33–48) occurs after the fall of Jerusalem to the Babylonian Empire in 586 BC. In these chapters, Ezekiel offers a different message, one of hope out of the bleakness of suffering. God gave Ezekiel a vision of a valley of dry bones springing to life with new flesh, a reminder that death is never the final judgment for God's people (Ezek. 37:11–14).

EZEKIEL

Ezekiel, whose name means "God will strengthen," ministered to the exiles in Nippur by the Kebar River near Babylon (Ezek. 1:1). His visions date from 593 BC (Ezek. 1:2) to 571 BC (Ezek. 29:17) during the reign of King Nebuchadnezzar of Babylon.

EZRA AND NEHEMIAH
Ezra 1–10; Nehemiah 1–13

The book of Ezra opens with the fulfillment of Jeremiah's prophecy: After seventy years of exile, the Jews would return to their homeland (Jer. 25:11–12; 29:10; Ezra 1:1). In 539 BC, the great Babylonian Empire had fallen to Persia. God worked in the heart of King Cyrus of Persia, causing him to decree that the Jews could return to Jerusalem and rebuild their temple (2 Chron. 36:22–23). But by this time, many exiles had laid down new roots in these foreign lands and chose to stay where they were. Still, thousands of Jews were determined to make the trek hundreds of miles to go to Judah and start over yet again.

Under the leadership of Zerubbabel and Joshua the high priest, the people laid a new foundation to rebuild the temple in Jerusalem that the Babylonians had razed (Ezra 3:10). However, not everyone was happy with this new building project, and construction stopped. God sent the prophets Haggai and Zechariah to call the people to renew their resolve to complete the temple (Ezra 5:1). With the prophets' urging, rebuilding resumed, and in 516 BC, seventy years after its destruction, a new temple was built—the visible sign that God was with his people (Ezra 6:14).

The narrative in the book of Ezra then fast-forwards about six decades and introduces a priest and scholar named Ezra. He led a large group of exiles on a four-month, nine-hundred-mile journey from Babylon to Jerusalem. Ezra instituted spiritual and social reforms to ensure that this new community in Jerusalem would obey God's law and avoid the sins that had led to the exile.

Meanwhile in the Persian capital of Susa, a Jewish man named Nehemiah served King Artaxerxes as his cupbearer (Neh. 1:11). Being a cupbearer to the king meant holding an influential position as a confidant of the king. When he heard that the walls of Jerusalem were in shambles,

Nehemiah, whose name means "the LORD comforts," was thrown into distress. He persuaded the king to let him go to Jerusalem at once and lead the rebuilding effort.

With Nehemiah's persistence, the city walls were rebuilt, and Ezra read God's law to the crowd and a renewed spirit of obedience to the Lord swept through the people. "Nehemiah said, 'This day is holy to our Lord. Do not grieve, for the joy of the LORD is your strength'" (Neh. 8:10). As Ezekiel had seen in his vision of dry bones being brought back to life, the people of God, who had suffered immensely and must have felt like dry dead bones, were given new life and a reason to celebrate in the joy of the Lord again.

EZRA

The book of Ezra tells the history of the exiles' return to Jerusalem in 538 BC, the rebuilding of the temple in 516 BC, and Ezra's reforms in Jerusalem about sixty years later. Chapters 1–6 occur before Ezra's time, with his own story beginning in chapter 7 and continuing through the end of the book. Ezra, who was a priest and a scribe, is believed to be the author of both the books of Ezra and Nehemiah.

NEHEMIAH

Nehemiah's story takes place at first in Susa, the capital of Persia, and then in Jerusalem where the people rebuilt the city walls, around 444–432 BC. The books of Ezra and Nehemiah were originally just one book. Nehemiah's story picks up where the book of Ezra leaves off. Together, Ezra the priest and Nehemiah the governor brought social and spiritual reforms to Jerusalem.

HAGGAI

The book of Haggai dates to around 520 BC, more than a decade after the first group of Jews returned to Jerusalem under Zerubbabel. Haggai's name means "festival" and his ministry is mentioned in Ezra 5:1; 6:14. Along with Zechariah, Haggai urged the people of Judah to continue rebuilding the temple.

ZECHARIAH

The book of Zechariah dates to around 520–518 BC. Zechariah's name means "the Lord remembers." He was a Jewish priest born in Babylon. He migrated to Jerusalem with the exiles who returned with Zerubbabel (Neh. 12:16). Along with Haggai, Zechariah urged the people to continue rebuilding the temple (Ezra 5:1; 6:14).

MALACHI

Malachi prophesied in Judah, possibly during the time of Ezra and Nehemiah in the 400s BC. His name means "messenger," but little else is known about him. The six prophetic speeches in the book of Malachi call for spiritual renewal among a people who had largely given up on God.

JOEL

It's not known when Joel prophesied, but some Bible scholars place his ministry either just before the exile in 586 BC or as late as the 400s–300s BC. Joel's name means "the Lord is God." The focus of Joel's book is to call the people of Judah to repent before the coming of the great and dreadful day of the Lord.

ESTHER

Esther's story is set in Susa, the capital of Persia, during the reign of King Xerxes (King Ahasuerus; 486–465 BC) and the drama takes place in the royal Persian court. At this time in biblical history, hundreds of miles away in Judah, exiled Jews had returned to Jerusalem and already rebuilt the temple of God. Yet many Jewish families had remained in foreign lands; Esther's family was one that stayed.

Chapters 1–2 tell how Esther became the queen of Persia and hid her Jewish identity. Chapters 3–5 explain how the lives of the Jews became threatened with annihilation. Chapters 6–10 show how Queen Esther revealed her Jewish identity and how she and her cousin Mordecai turned the tables and the Jews were spared, and then established the holiday of Purim (Feast of Lots) to commemorate the victory.

For over one thousand years God had spoken to the Jewish people. From Moses to Malachi they had heard, repeatedly, the message of God's faithful covenant love for them coupled with his call for them to be faithful in return. Then, seeming silence descended as four hundred years passed between the prophet Malachi in the Old Testament and the angelic visits Luke describes in the first chapter of his gospel in the New Testament. This gap is known as the intertestamental period—the time between the testaments.

> *"The people were waiting expectantly and were all wondering in their hearts ..."*
>
> LUKE 3:15

But these four centuries were anything but quiet on the world scene. Major shifts between powers and cultures took place during this time. In the early fourth century BC, the powerful Persian Empire succumbed to the swift and seemingly unstoppable Greek army under Alexander the Great. After Alexander's death at a young age, the land of Israel was dominated by the empires left in Alexander's wake: the Ptolemies and Seleucids. In the second century BC, however, the Jews experienced a time of independence when the Jewish Maccabees defeated the Seleucids and reclaimed Jerusalem and its temple. Their rededication of the temple came to be celebrated as the Jewish festival of Hanukkah, the Feast of Dedication (John 10:22). Yet in time, the fast-growing Roman Empire conquered much of the Near East, establishing itself as the ruling power up to and through the time of Jesus.

HOPE FOR A MESSIAH

Life for the Jewish people under Roman rule in the first century AD can be characterized by extremes. On one hand, they were given freedom to work, live, and worship. But on the other hand, they were also constantly reminded that they were not truly free. Roman soldiers occupied their land continually. The burden of high taxes paid to Rome drove many people into poverty or slavery.

The Jews longed for a day when they could truly be free, something that the prophets had promised with the coming of the Messiah. (The term *messiah* is Hebrew for "anointed one," called so because the king was set apart by being anointed with oil poured over his head.) As Isaiah had prophesied: "He will be called Wonderful Counselor, Mighty God, Everlasting Father, Prince of Peace.... He will reign on David's throne and over his kingdom, establishing and upholding it with justice and righteousness" (Isa. 9:6–7).

Most Jews held to the belief in a coming Messiah. However, they disagreed about what they thought this Messiah would do. In general, they believed that the Messiah would be a human who was aided in some way by God to do amazing, miraculous things—a king of Israel and descendant of King David. However, some, perhaps influenced by more secular thinking at the time, held that the Messiah was more of a concept that would enable the nation of Israel to come together and overthrow the rulers oppressing them.

Whatever their understanding, there was a general longing for a conquering king who would come and crush their oppressors and free them, establishing Israel as a prosperous nation once again. So when a miracle-working, humble young man from Nazareth burst onto the scene challenging the established religious authorities and loving even Roman authority figures, even his own disciples were confused. They had not envisioned a Messiah like him; one who would fulfill a promise from God given not only to David, but all the way back to Abraham—a king who rescues not only the Jews, but the whole world, from our greatest enemies: sin and death.

BIRTH OF CHRIST
Matthew 1–2; Luke 1–2

One would expect the arrival of the Messiah to have been a major, national event for the Jewish people, right?

It was anything but.

> "For God so loved the world that he gave his one and only Son, that whoever believes in him shall not perish but have eternal life."
>
> JOHN 3:16

Of the four gospels, only Luke and Matthew say anything about the birth of Jesus. Both gospel writers describe angelic visits to Joseph and Mary—a kind of heavenly heads up to a humble, unsuspecting couple. The angelic message was straightforward, yet astounding: Mary, a betrothed virgin, would give birth to the Messiah (*Christ* in Greek). He would be called Jesus—a variant of the name Joshua, which means "salvation"—because he would "save his people from their sins" (Matt. 1:21). He would also be called Son of the Most High and *Immanuel*, meaning "God with us" (Matt. 1:23). He would establish a kingdom that would never end (Luke 1:32–33).

On the night of Jesus' birth in the town of Bethlehem, the city of David, only a small band of stunned shepherds came to see the newborn baby—and this was only because they'd just heard about the event from an enthusiastic multitude of angels. Some days (possibly weeks) later, magi or "wise men" from the east showed up at the house where Jesus was. They worshiped him, showered him with gifts, and left. Had it not been for these two groups, it's doubtful that anyone but a handful of people would have been aware that the Messiah had just been born. In fact, it was only when the magi stopped first in Jerusalem asking questions about a "newborn king" that King Herod the Great became paranoid and concocted a murderous plot to eliminate all young boys in and around Bethlehem. Warned in a dream about Herod's intentions, Joseph and Mary fled to Egypt with Jesus. After Herod died, they settled in Nazareth of Galilee.

The gospels tell us very little about Jesus' childhood. What we do know is that Jesus grew up in Nazareth of Galilee, had siblings (Matt. 13:55), probably learned the business of carpentry from Joseph (Mark 6:3), and at one Passover in Jerusalem, he astounded the teachers in the temple with his understanding of the Hebrew Scriptures (Luke 2:41–50). Luke explains that Jesus "grew and became strong; he was filled with wisdom, and the grace of God was on him" (Luke 2:40).

EARLY MINISTRY
Matthew 3–4; Mark 1; Luke 3–4; John 1–4

When Jesus was about the age of thirty, many people were streaming into the wilderness northeast of Jerusalem to listen to a fiery, mesmerizing prophet named John, who was calling people to repent and prepare for the Messiah's coming. John was baptizing in the Jordan River all those who were receptive to his message. When some people began asking if he was the promised Messiah, John quickly insisted that he was only a lowly servant preparing the way for God's anointed (Luke 3:16).

Shortly after this, Jesus, the carpenter from Nazareth, stepped out of the crowd. John pointed at him and declared that he was "the Lamb of God, who takes away the sin of the world" (John 1:29). Jesus was baptized by John to identify with John and his message and the sinners Jesus had come to save. At Jesus' baptism, he was anointed by the Holy Spirit coming down from heaven in the form of a dove and affirmed as the Son of God by an audible voice from heaven. Then, immediately, he was led by the Holy Spirit into the wilderness to overcome the temptations of the devil (Mark 1:12–13). After these events, Jesus began a three-year public ministry. He gathered a few disciples and quickly began to shock them with his words and works.

TEACHINGS AND MIRACLES
Matthew 5–20; Mark 2–10; Luke 5–19; John 5–12

Jesus taught constantly, sharing the deep truths of God. He taught in synagogues, the temple courts, people's homes, and outdoor settings. He preached in all sorts of contexts to huge crowds and small groups. He often seized on "chance" encounters to illustrate and explain spiritual truths to spiritually curious individuals. His authoritative words always left people scratching their heads in amazement: "The crowds were amazed at his teaching, because he taught as one who had authority, and not as their teachers of the law" (Matt. 7:28–29).

As Jesus was preaching the gospel and teaching about the kingdom of God, he punctuated his ministry with breathtaking miracles. His ministry involved "healing every disease and sickness among the people" (Matt. 4:23). Jesus gave sight to the blind and hearing to the deaf. He corrected deformities and cured paralysis. Sometimes he healed by physically touching the sick, and sometimes the sick found healing by simply touching him. On some occasions, he made people whole by speaking a word from a distance.

These wondrous acts weren't tricks performed to impress others or to draw a crowd. On one level, they stemmed from the fathomless compassion of Jesus. When he saw hurting, needy people, he was moved to alleviate their suffering. On another level, these miracles functioned as "signs" (John 2:11). They authenticated his message. In other words, his miracles demonstrated the truth of his claims to be the God-sent Savior of the world.

Almost from the start of his public ministry, Jesus was immensely popular with the masses. Yet the longer he ministered, the more he infuriated the Jewish religious leaders. From the beginning, Jesus made it clear that he had not come "to abolish the Law or the Prophets ... but to fulfill them" (Matt. 5:17). He always displayed the utmost reverence for God's Word. However, he had zero patience for man-made religious rules. He riled the Pharisees, telling them, "You have a fine way of setting aside the commands of God in order to observe your own traditions!" (Mark 7:9). Jesus also raised eyebrows in the way he elevated women in a culture that viewed them as second-class citizens (John 4). People were scandalized by the way he honored little children and treated social outcasts with dignity (Matt. 8:3; 19:13–15; Mark 2:16).

Mostly, however, Jesus shattered the public's prevailing understanding of the Messiah. *When would God restore the kingdom to Israel? Where was the deliverer who, in the spirit and manner of King David, would galvanize the people, lead a revolt, and drive the Roman pagans from the Jewish homeland?* These were the questions on every heart and tongue. Many became convinced that Jesus would be this military deliverer. Yet when they tried to push Jesus in this direction, he resisted. He was clear about his mission: "For I have come down from heaven not to do my will but to do the will of him who sent me" (John 6:38). According to Jesus, God's will for him was to preach the good news of God's kingdom, call sinners to repentance, testify to the truth, bring light to a dark world, and drive out the devil. Jesus was the divine King and Messiah, but he was one who "did not come to be served, but to serve" (Mark 10:45).

JOURNEY TO THE CROSS
Matthew 21–27; Mark 11–15; Luke 19–23; John 12–19

During his three-year ministry, Jesus made (and accepted) extraordinary claims about himself. Jesus even declared himself and God "one"—a statement that outraged his

Jewish listeners. They considered such words blasphemous, and they almost stoned him on the spot (John 10:30–33). Jesus had to know that such claims would cost him his life. In fact, he told his disciples exactly what would happen to him: "We are going up to Jerusalem, and the Son of Man will be delivered over to the chief priests and the teachers of the law. They will condemn him to death and will hand him over to the Gentiles to be mocked and flogged and crucified" (Matt. 20:18–19). Yet he headed to Jerusalem, straight to the cross that awaited him there—knowingly, willingly, and sacrificially.

Starting with Jesus' arrival in Jerusalem, all four gospels focus extensively on his final week:

Sunday: Jesus' triumphal entry into Jerusalem on what has come to be known as Palm Sunday raised the crowd's messianic hopes yet again. With palm branches in hand, people lined the road shouting *hosanna*, which means "salvation at last!"

Monday: Jesus moved through the temple courts, angrily turning over the tables of corrupt money changers and merchants.

Tuesday: His disruptive acts from the day before prompted fierce arguments with the religious leaders at the temple.

Later, on the Mount of Olives east of Jerusalem, Jesus prepared his followers for his departure. He told them about the coming signs of the end times, his glorious return, and the ultimate triumph of God's kingdom.

Wednesday: The gospels don't specifically mention what happened on Wednesday, but we do know that sometime during the week the religious leaders plotted against Jesus with the help of a co-conspirator, Judas Iscariot, one of Jesus' twelve disciples.

Thursday: On Thursday night, Jesus gathered the disciples in an upstairs room to share the Passover meal one final time with them. He used the occasion to institute a new meal—the Lord's Supper. This meal would commemorate his body broken and his blood spilled as a sacrifice. Jesus explained to his disciples: "This is my blood of the covenant, which is poured out for many for the forgiveness of sins" (Matt. 26:27–28); and "This [bread] is my body given for you; do this in remembrance of me" (Luke 22:19).

Just after that last supper with his disciples, Jesus went to the garden of Gethsemane with Peter, James, and John to pray. Jesus was visibly in deep anguish as he contemplated the horrific death he would soon face (Luke 22:44). Through prayer, he was given strength to carry out the Father's plan: "Father, if you are willing, take this cup from me; yet not my will, but yours be done" (Luke 22:42). Strengthened with holy resolve, he rose, just in time to meet Judas and the mob who had come to arrest him.

Friday: In the wee hours of Friday morning, the Jewish and Roman authorities sent Jesus to illegal nighttime trials. Pontius Pilate, who was the Roman prefect of Judea, sentenced Jesus to death.

Jesus was stripped and flogged mercilessly by Roman soldiers skilled in the brutal business of execution. The men took turns punching him, spitting on him, and mocking him with a purple robe and a crown of thorns. Then they led him to Golgotha—an infamous execution site, along a major thoroughfare outside the city walls—where they hammered him to a cross. Between two convicted criminals, Jesus died a gruesome, agonizing death. Yet even then, while on the cross, Jesus prayed for his executioners: "Father, forgive them, for they do not know what they are doing" (Luke 23:34). Mark records that Jesus was crucified on the "third hour" (9:00 a.m.) and died six hours later on the "ninth hour" (3:00 p.m.) (Mark 15:25, 34).

Shortly before the beginning of the Sabbath day, which started at sunset on Friday, the Roman soldiers overseeing the crucifixion realized that Jesus was already dead. (Death by crucifixion could sometimes take days.) The soldiers removed his lifeless body from the cross and, on the orders of Pilate, released it to Joseph of Arimathea who wrapped Christ's body in "a clean linen cloth, and placed it in his own new tomb that he had cut out of the rock" (Matt. 27:59–60).

THE EMPTY TOMB AND HIS PROMISE TO COME AGAIN
Matthew 28; Mark 16; Luke 24; John 20–21; Acts 1

Early Sunday morning, several women who were followers of Jesus arrived at his tomb, hoping for an opportunity to properly anoint his body. What they found in the tomb left them shocked, stunned, and bewildered, but ultimately overjoyed. The tomb was open and empty! The great stone that had sealed the tomb had been rolled away. Grave linens were lying loose. Angels appeared, saying matter-of-factly, "He is not here; he has risen, just as he said" (Matt. 28:6). And then, the followers of Jesus, both singly and in groups, had actual encounters with the resurrected Jesus—not a phantom or a spirit, but a back-from-the-dead Savior they could touch.

About six weeks after the crucifixion, the resurrected Christ gathered his disciples one final time and told them their mission—the Great Commission: "Go and make disciples of all nations, baptizing them in the name of the Father and of the Son and of the Holy Spirit" (Matt. 28:19). Then they watched as he rose into heaven. As they stood there staring, angels told them, "Men of Galilee ... why do you stand here looking into the sky? This same Jesus, who has been taken from you into heaven, will come back in the same way you have seen him go into heaven" (Acts 1:11).

That message wasn't only for a handful of disciples in Galilee two millennia ago. That message is for all believers in Jesus—then, now, and in the future. Believers in Jesus wait and watch eagerly for his return because he will "come at an hour when you do not expect him" (Matt. 24:44).

The Four Biographies of Jesus

The first four books of the New Testament are known as the gospels ("good news") and named after their authors: Matthew, Mark, Luke, and John. While the gospels of Matthew, Mark, and Luke contain the most similar stories, each of the four biographies of Jesus present his life and ministry from a different perspective.

Modern biographies typically narrate the events of a person's life in the order in which they occurred, but biographies in the time of Jesus were quite different. Though ancient biographers put big events into historical sequence, they didn't place every activity in chronological order. Instead, it was more important to develop an accurate picture of the person's character. While the gospels provide us with very similar stories about Jesus, the order of some events across the four gospels doesn't always match up. That's because the main purpose of each gospel was to show the reader who Jesus was and what his life means for us.

MATTHEW

This gospel was written by Matthew (Levi) a tax collector who became one of the twelve disciples (Matt. 9:9). It was written in the AD 60s or later. As the most *prophetic* gospel, Matthew quotes extensively from the Old Testament and focuses on the teachings of Jesus the Messiah King. This gospel covers the birth of Jesus and his public ministry through the resurrection appearances.

MARK

This gospel was written by John Mark an early believer and helper to the apostles Paul and Peter (Acts 12:12; Col. 4:10). It's believed to have been the earliest of the four gospels, written possibly in the AD 50s. As the most *practical* gospel, Mark focuses on the actions of Jesus the divine Servant and highlights the humanity of Jesus (Mark 3:5; 6:34; 14:33–34). It's a fast paced narrative starting with Jesus' baptism and concluding with the resurrection.

LUKE

This gospel was likely written about AD 60–62 by Luke, a gentile missionary-doctor and colleague of the apostle Paul (Col. 4:14). As the most *historical* gospel, Luke provides a detailed account of the life and ministry of Jesus, demonstrating Jesus' character and virtue. He focuses on Jesus as the divine Son of Man.

Luke begins his gospel with the birth of John the Baptist and concludes with the ascension of Jesus into heaven.

JOHN

This gospel was written by John, who, along with Peter and James, was part of the "inner circle" of Jesus' disciples (Matt. 4:21). It was written in the later part of the first century. As the most *theological* gospel, John focuses on Jesus as the Son of God incarnate. This book contains lengthy teachings of Jesus and detailed miracle accounts (some not found in the other gospels). John concludes with Jesus' resurrection appearances.

How Long Was Jesus' Ministry?

One way to measure the length of Jesus' public ministry is by counting the number of Passovers in John's gospel. John mentions four Passovers (John 2:13; 5:1; 6:4; 13:1); the first one very early in Jesus' ministry and the last one in Jesus' final week in Jerusalem. (The festival in John 5:1 is believed to be either Passover itself or another festival near the Passover season.) This means that Jesus' ministry continued for at least three years.

LIFE OF JESUS TIME LINE

BIRTH & CHILDHOOD

ANNUNCIATION The angel Gabriel tells Mary that she will bear a son through the Holy Spirit. Luke 1:26–38

The angel Gabriel tells Joseph to take Mary as his wife. Matt. 1:18–25

4 BC **BIRTH OF CHRIST** Jesus is born in Bethlehem. Luke 2:1–7

Shepherds visit Jesus lying in the manger. Luke 2:8–20

At the temple, Jesus is recognized as the Messiah. Luke 2:21–38

Magi from the east visit Jesus. Matt. 2:1–12

Joseph, Mary, and Jesus flee to Egypt to escape King Herod. They return to Nazareth after Herod's death. Matt. 2:13–23

Age 12 Jesus amazes teachers at the temple. Luke 2:41–52

EARLY MINISTRY

BAPTISM John the Baptist baptizes Jesus in the Jordan River. Matt. 3:13–17; Mark 1:9–11; Luke 3:21–22

Age 30; AD 27 Jesus resists Satan's temptations in the wilderness. Matt. 4:1–11; Mark 1:12–13; Luke 4:1–13

Time line dates are approximate.

FIRST MIRACLE Jesus turns water into wine at a wedding in Cana. John 2:1–12

Passover #1 ⊙ Jesus cleanses the temple. John 2:13–25

● In Jerusalem, Nicodemus and Jesus converse about the kingdom of God. John 3:1–21

● Jesus meets the Samaritan woman at a well in Sychar. John 4:1–42

MINISTRY PRIMARILY IN GALILEE

● In Cana, Jesus heals an official's son from a distance. John 4:46–54

● Beside the Sea of Galilee, Jesus calls his disciples. Matt. 4:18–22; Mark 1:16–20; Luke 5:1–11

● In Capernaum, Jesus heals and forgives a paralyzed man. Matt. 9:1–8; Mark 2:1–12; Luke 5:17–26

● Jesus dines with "sinners." Matt. 9:9–13; Mark 2:13–17; Luke 5:27–32

● Jesus heals a man at the pool of Bethesda. John 5:1–47

Passover #2 ⊙ **SERMON ON THE MOUNT** From a hillside in Galilee, Jesus teaches with authority. Matt. 5:1–7:29; Luke 6:20–49; 11:1–13; 16:16–17

● Jesus heals a centurion's servant in Cana. Matt. 8:5–13; Luke 7:1–10

● In the city of Nain, Jesus raises a widow's son from the dead. Luke 7:11–17

● Pharisees accuse Jesus of being in league with Satan. Matt. 12:22–37; Mark 3:20–30; Luke 11:14–28

● Jesus calms a storm on the Sea of Galilee. Matt. 8:23–27; Mark 4:35–41; Luke 8:22–25

● Jesus casts demons out of a man and into pigs. Matt. 8:28–34; Mark 5:1–20; Luke 8:26–39

- Jesus raises Jairus's daughter and heals a woman who touches his cloak. Matt. 9:18–26; Mark 5:21–43; Luke 8:40–56

Passover #3 ◉ **JESUS FEEDS THE 5,000** with just a few fish and loaves of bread near Bethsaida. Matt. 14:13–21; Mark 6:30–44; Luke 9:10–17; John 6:1–15

- Jesus walks on water on the Sea of Galilee. Matt. 14:22–36; Mark 6:45–56; John 6:16–21

- Jesus teaches, "I am the bread of life." John 6:22–71

- Jesus heals a Canaanite woman's daughter in the region of Tyre and Sidon. Matt. 15:21–28; Mark 7:24–30

- Jesus feeds the 4,000. Matt. 15:29–39; Mark 8:1–10

- Jesus heals a blind man at Bethsaida. Mark 8:22–26

- Peter calls Jesus the Messiah/Christ. Matt. 16:13–20; Mark 8:27–30; Luke 9:18–21

◉ **TRANSFIGURATION** Jesus is seen in glory. Matt. 17:1–13; Mark 9:2–13; Luke 9:28–36

MINISTRY JUDEA & PEREA

- In Jerusalem, Jesus spares a woman caught in adultery. John 7:53–8:11*

- Jesus sends out the 72. Luke 10:1–24

- Jesus visits the home of Martha and Mary in Bethany. Luke 10:38–42

- Jesus heals a crippled woman on the Sabbath. Luke 13:10–17

- Jesus heals a man born blind. John 9:1–41

- Opponents try to stone Jesus for blasphemy. John 10:22–42

* Some early manuscripts don't have these verses.

- Jesus mourns over Jerusalem. Matt. 22:37–39; Luke 13:31–35

- Jesus dines with Pharisees and heals a man with dropsy. Luke 14:1–24

- In Bethany, Jesus raises Lazarus from the dead. John 11:1–44

- The Sanhedrin plots to kill Jesus. John 11:45–57

- A rich young ruler and Jesus converse about eternal life. Matt. 19:16–30; Mark 10:17–31; Luke 18:18–30

- In Jericho, Jesus heals Bartimaeus and another blind man. Matt. 20:29–34; Mark 10:46–52; Luke 18:35–43

- Jesus visits Zacchaeus, a tax collector in Jericho. Luke 19:1–27

- In Bethany, Mary anoints Jesus' feet with perfume. Matt. 26:6–13; Mark 14:3–9; John 12:1–8

JESUS' LAST WEEK

AD 30
Sunday

TRIUMPHAL ENTRY Jesus enters Jerusalem.
Matt. 21:1–11; Mark 11:1–11; Luke 19:28–44; John 12:12–19

Monday

Jesus cleanses the temple. Matt. 21:12–16;
Mark 11:15–19; Luke 19:45–46

Tuesday

Pharisees and Jesus dispute in the temple courts. Matt. 22:15–45; Mark 12:13–27, 35–40;
Luke 20:20–47

Jesus commends the widow's offering.
Mark 12:41–44; Luke 21:1–4

OLIVET DISCOURSE Jesus teaches his disciples on the Mount of Olives. Matt. 24:1–25:46; Mark 13:1–37;
Luke 21:5–38

Wednesday**	●	Judas Iscariot agrees to betray Jesus. Matt. 26:1–5, 14–16; Mark 14:1–2, 10–11; Luke 22:1–6
Thursday	●	Jesus washes his disciples' feet. John 13:1–17
Passover #4	◉	**LAST SUPPER** Jesus and his disciples share a final meal in an upper room in Jerusalem. Matt. 26:17–30; Mark 14:12–26; Luke 22:7–30; John 13:18–30
	●	Jesus predicts Peter's denials. Matt. 26:31–35; Mark 14:27–31; Luke 22:31–38; John 13:31–38
	●	Jesus prays in the garden of Gethsemane. Matt. 26:36–46; Mark 14:32–42; Luke 22:39–46
Midnight	●	While still in Gethsemane, Jesus is arrested when Judas betrays him. Matt. 26:47–56; Mark 14:43–52; Luke 22:47–53; John 18:1–12
Friday	●	Jesus stands trial before Annas, Caiaphas, and the Sanhedrin. Matt. 26:57–68; Mark 14:53–65; Luke 22:54; John 18:13–14, 19–24
	●	Peter disowns Jesus three times. Matt. 26:69–75; Mark 14:66–72; Luke 22:54–62; John 18:15–18, 25–27
Daybreak	●	The Sanhedrin condemns Jesus. Matt. 27:1–2; Mark 15:1; Luke 22:63–71
	●	Jesus stands trial before Pilate at Herod's Palace and Herod Antipas at his palace. Matt. 27:11–26; Mark 15:2–15; Luke 23:1–25; John 18:28–19:16
	●	Soldiers beat Jesus and mock him with a crown of thorns. Matt. 27:27–31; Mark 15:16–20; John 19:1–3
	●	Simon is forced to carry Jesus' cross. Matt. 27:32; Mark 15:21; Luke 23:26–32; John 19:17
9:00 a.m.	◉	**CRUCIFIXION** Jesus is nailed to the cross at Golgotha. Matt. 27:33–44; Mark 15:22–32; Luke 23:33–38; John 19:18–24

** The gospels don't mention Wednesday specifically, but Luke 21:37–38 suggests that Jesus taught in the temple courts on this day. Judas and the religious leaders may have plotted together on this day.

| 3:00 p.m. | ● | **Jesus dies on the cross.** Matt. 27:45–56; Mark 15:33–41; Luke 23:44–49; John 19:28–37 |

| Sunset | ● | **Jesus' body is placed in the tomb.** Matt. 27:57–61; Mark 15:42–47; Luke 23:50–56; John 19:38–42 |

| Saturday | ● | **Roman guard is posted at the tomb.** Matt. 27:62–66 |

Sunday ◉ **RESURRECTION** Women find the tomb of Jesus empty. Matt. 28:1–8; Mark 16:1–8; Luke 24:1–8; John 20:1–2

● Peter and John run to the tomb and also find it empty. Luke 24:9–12; John 20:3–10

APPEARANCES & ASCENSION

● **Jesus appears to Mary Magdalene and other women.** Matt. 28:8–10; Mark 16:9–11*; John 20:11–18

● **Jesus appears to two disciples on the road to Emmaus.** Mark 16:12–13*; Luke 24:13–35

● **Jesus appears to his disciples twice.** Mark 16:14*; Luke 24:36–49; John 20:19–31

● **On the shore of the Sea of Galilee, Jesus eats with his disciples after a miraculous catch of fish.** John 21:1–14

● **Jesus restores Peter: "Feed my sheep."** John 21:15–25

◉ **GREAT COMMISSION** "Go and make disciples of all nations." Matt. 28:16–20

40 days after the Resurrection ◉ **ASCENSION** Jesus ascends to heaven from the Mount of Olives. Mark 16:19–20*; Luke 24:50–53; Acts 1:3–11

Though Bible scholars today differ about the precise sequence of events in the life of Jesus, we have tried to ensure that the material presented here is consistent with widely held interpretations of the basic chronology in the gospels.

THE APOSTLES

HOLY SPIRIT AT PENTECOST
Acts 1–3

On the heels of the four gospels in the New Testament comes the lengthy book of Acts. The narrative of Acts begins with Christ's ascension into heaven. Before he departed, he told his closest disciples, "You will receive power when the Holy Spirit comes on you; and you will be my witnesses in Jerusalem, and in all Judea and Samaria, and to the ends of the earth" (Acts 1:8).

> "Salvation is found in no one else, for there is no other name given under heaven by which we must be saved."
>
> ACTS 4:12

As instructed, the disciples got to work, praying, and waiting in Jerusalem. But they didn't have to wait long. While Jews from all over were gathered in Jerusalem for the festival of Pentecost, the Holy Spirit of God came upon the followers of Jesus like a hurricane (Acts 2:2–4). The believers were empowered to share the truth of God with all those foreign visitors in languages ("tongues") that they themselves had never learned! The apostle Peter seized the moment and gave a short sermon to the crowd. As a result, three thousand people repented of their sins, put their faith in Jesus, and were baptized.

This new spiritual community, called the church, was fiercely devoted to the apostles' teaching. They shared a common faith, a common life, and a common mission. They worshiped wholeheartedly, prayed fervently, and saw God do miraculous things through the apostles. As a result, the whole city of Jerusalem was in awe.

PERSECUTION AND THE CHURCH
Acts 4–9

Not surprisingly, this rapid, new movement was soon met with backlash. Apostles Peter and John were arrested and brought before the Sanhedrin, the same court that only weeks before had condemned Jesus to death (Matt. 26:59–68). Filled with the Holy Spirit, Peter boldly preached the gospel to them, declaring that salvation is found in no one else besides Jesus (Acts 4:12). Threatened, but ultimately released, Peter and John ramped up their efforts to share the good news, and the church continued to grow.

The more the Jewish leaders cracked down, the more the church spoke up. Nothing could deter Christ's followers, not threats, floggings, or even death. One church leader, Stephen, was dragged outside Jerusalem and stoned to death for testifying about Jesus. Stephen's death sparked a wave of violent persecution against the church. Believers in Jesus fled Jerusalem in droves. But ironically, this only meant that the gospel was advancing. Opposition in Jerusalem sent them into Judea and Samaria, just as Jesus had said would happen (Acts 1:8).

One of the chief engineers of the persecution campaign against the church was a young man named Saul (also called Paul). About five years after Stephen was martyred in Jerusalem (Saul had been there for that; Acts 7:58; 8:1), Saul set his sights on Damascus, a city northeast of Jerusalem. He was headed to Damascus to arrest believers in Jesus who had fled persecution in Jerusalem. Saul set out to apprehend followers of Jesus, but on the way, it was he who was "apprehended by Christ Jesus" (Phil. 3:12 KJV). A great light flashed from heaven, he fell to the ground, and the risen Lord revealed the truth: "I am Jesus, whom you are persecuting" (Acts 9:5). Physically blinded by the experience, Saul arrived in Damascus where the Lord directed a man named Ananias to go to him and restore his sight. Confronted, then converted by Jesus, Saul joined the very movement he had tried to abolish!

PETER'S MISSION
Acts 10–12

Meanwhile, God was using Peter to open the door of salvation—and of the church—to those outside the Jewish community. God sent Peter to the home of Cornelius, a Roman centurion and a gentile (non-Jew). There, Peter saw the Holy Spirit fill the gentile believers, and he was convinced: "I now realize how true it is that God does not show favoritism but accepts from every nation the one who fears him and does what is right" (Acts 10:34–35).

Soon, there was a growing and thriving community of gentile believers in Antioch of Syria (Acts 11:19–30). In fact, it was in this city that the followers of Jesus were first called *Christians*, and it was from here that Paul (Saul) launched his missionary efforts to reach the world with the gospel.

PAUL'S JOURNEYS
Acts 13–28

About half of the chapters in Acts focus on Paul's journeys. For his first missionary outreach, Paul teamed up with Barnabas and for a short time with John Mark. By the Holy Spirit's leading, they took the gospel to the island of Cyprus, then to cities in the south-central region of Asia Minor (modern day Turkey).

On his second missionary journey, Paul was accompanied by Silas, and they were later joined by Timothy, a husband-and-wife team Priscilla and Aquila, as well as Luke the author of the gospel of Luke and Acts. Paul headed north and then west through Asia Minor and Greece, this apostolic team strengthening believers and establishing churches everywhere they went.

On his third journey, Paul retraced his steps, revisiting cities he'd previously evangelized and church congregations he had helped plant. While on this mission, Paul wrote his longest epistle (letter) in the New Testament—the epistle to the Romans. This was Paul's comprehensive explanation of God's plan of salvation.

Later, when Paul was in Jerusalem, he was falsely accused of defiling the temple, arrested, and sent to prison. He was held in prison two years awaiting trial. Nevertheless, he shared his faith with various high-ranking officials while he waited in chains. Paul was eventually put on a ship headed to Rome to appeal his case to Caesar. This journey would be the farthest he had traveled—to Rome, the epicenter of the Greco-Roman world, far from where the church had begun in Jerusalem, Judea, and Samaria (Acts 1:8).

When he arrived in Rome, Paul was placed under house arrest to await yet another trial. This is where the narrative of Acts ends, with Paul using the difficult situation he was in as an opportunity to tell others about salvation in Jesus: "He proclaimed the kingdom of God and taught about the Lord Jesus Christ—with all boldness and without hindrance!" (Acts 28:30–31).

ACTS

Acts tells the story (or the "acts") of the Holy Spirit working in the first Christians to spread the good news of Jesus from Jerusalem, Judea, Samaria, and to the world, about AD 30–62. Written by Luke, Acts picks up where the gospel of Luke left off, with Jesus' ascension into heaven. The first twelve chapters focus on Peter and the apostles in Jerusalem, Judea, and Samaria. The remaining chapters detail Paul's missionary journeys.

JAMES

James, the brother of Jesus, wrote this letter to Jewish believers scattered across the Roman Empire, about AD 49. James was martyred in Jerusalem about thirteen years later in AD 62. This short and very practical letter encourages believers to have an active, living faith that perseveres through all kinds of trials.

GALATIANS

Possibly the earliest of Paul's epistles, this letter was written to churches in Galatia from Paul's home base of Antioch of Syria, about AD 49. Paul defends his authority as an apostle and argues that the true gospel teaches that justification is by faith alone; people are saved by faith, not by good works or by obeying religious laws.

1 THESSALONIANS

Paul wrote his first letter to the church in Thessalonica during his second missionary journey, about AD 50–51. Paul and Silas had earlier been forced to leave Thessalonica by an angry mob (see Acts 17:1–10). Paul spends the first part of this letter explaining his actions and absence. Then, he encourages believers to live holy lives, despite persecution, because Christ is coming again.

2 THESSALONIANS

Paul wrote his second letter to the church in Thessalonica during his second missionary journey, about AD 50–51, only six months after the first letter. This second letter echoes many themes from the first letter. Paul clears up misunderstandings the Thessalonians had about the second coming of Christ and about those who pass away before Christ's return.

1 CORINTHIANS

Paul wrote this letter to the church in Corinth during his third missionary journey, about AD 55–56. He had founded the Corinthian church just a few years earlier on his second missionary trip (Acts 18:1–11). Paul addresses problems in the church, like division and immorality. He tells believers to love one another and to use their spiritual gifts to build each other up, for they are all one body in Christ.

2 CORINTHIANS

Paul wrote this letter to the church in Corinth during his third missionary journey, about AD 56, not long after 1 Corinthians. The problems addressed in 1 Corinthians were apparently not resolved. So, in this letter, Paul reinforces what he had taught earlier, and he offers a passionate defense of his ministry in the face of many attacks.

ROMANS

Paul wrote this letter to the church in Rome at the end of his third missionary journey, about AD 57. This was just before he went to Jerusalem, where he was taken captive and eventually brought to Rome in chains. This is Paul's longest and most theological epistle. He discusses crucial topics of the Christian faith: law and the Spirit; sin and righteousness; condemnation and salvation.

EPHESIANS

Paul wrote this letter to the church in Ephesus while under house arrest in Rome, about AD 60–62. Paul had spent two years with the Ephesian Christians on his third missionary journey, so he knew their struggles up close. They faced tremendous pressure to participate in the sinfulness of their pagan surroundings. Paul urges them to resist that pressure and to seize the riches of God's grace in Christ.

PHILIPPIANS

Paul wrote this letter to the church in Philippi while under house arrest in Rome, about AD 60–62. Many people had become Christians in Philippi when Paul had visited the city on his second missionary journey. Paul urges believers to "have the same mindset as Christ" (Phil. 2:5) and to live humbly toward one another in unity.

COLOSSIANS

Paul wrote this letter to the church in Colossae while under house arrest in Rome, about AD 60–62. Paul intended the letter also to be read to the nearby church in Laodicea (Col. 4:16). Paul argues against a legalism that requires gentile Christians to follow Jewish religious laws. He dispels false teachings by emphasizing the supremacy of Christ.

PHILEMON

Paul wrote this letter to Philemon, a wealthy leader in the church in Colossae, while under house arrest in Rome, about AD 60–62. This letter was probably sent along with the epistle of Colossians. This is Paul's shortest epistle, only 25 verses. In it, he directly appeals to Philemon to accept a runaway slave, Onesimus, back as a brother in Christ: "You might have him back forever—no longer as a slave, but ... as a dear brother" (Philem. 15–16). Verse 10 suggests that Onesimus had met Paul and became a Christian, and apparently wished for reconciliation with his old master.

THE APOSTLE PAUL
1 and 2 Timothy; Titus

> "For the Spirit God gave us does not make us timid, but gives power, love and self-discipline. So do not be ashamed of the testimony about our Lord."
>
> 2 TIMOTHY 1:7–8

What happened in the decades following Acts can be pieced together from clues in the epistles written during this time, Christian tradition, and the historical record. While we don't know everything about Paul's final years, the most accepted theory is that after two years of house arrest, Paul was released and allowed to travel again. From Paul's epistles written to Timothy and Titus, we know that he visited churches in Macedonia, Troas, Miletus, Crete, and Nicopolis (1 Tim. 1:3; 2 Tim. 4:13, 20; Titus 1:5; 3:12). (The early church leader Clement said that Paul did fulfill his desire to go Spain, expressed in Romans 15:28, but whether the visit actually took place remains uncertain.)

But after just a few years, Paul ended up in prison in Rome. By the time he returned to the city, Emperor Nero had already begun a brutal persecution of Christians. Paul's imprisonment this time was not house arrest. Rather, it's believed to have been in the cold, infamous Mamertine Prison, where the apostle Peter might also have been held. Some information about Paul's final days can be gleaned from his second letter to Timothy, written from prison.

From this personal, heartfelt epistle, we know that Paul was visited by Onesiphorus, who "often refreshed me and was not ashamed of my chains" (2 Tim. 1:16–17). But we also know that Paul had been abandoned by many Christians when he stood trial (2 Tim. 4:10, 16). Luke alone was still with Paul, although Paul expressed the hope that he would see John Mark again when Timothy came to visit (2 Tim. 4:11).

Historical evidence suggests that Paul was executed in Rome, around AD 66–68. According to tradition, he was beheaded on the Ostian Way, a road just outside the city. (Peter, too, is believed to have been martyred during this time under Nero's persecutions, possibly being crucified upside down.)

The Lord had chosen Paul on the road to Damascus some thirty years prior, and Paul had chosen to follow the Lord wherever he led, even when that path led to suffering. In Paul's last epistle, he wrote, "The time for my departure is near. I have fought the good fight, I have finished the race, I have kept the faith. Now there is in store for me the crown of righteousness, which the Lord, the righteous Judge, will award to me on that day—and not only to me, but also to all who have longed for his appearing" (2 Tim. 4:6–8).

1 TIMOTHY

Paul wrote this letter to Timothy, a young pastor in Ephesus, about AD 62–66. Paul gives instructions to Timothy about proper worship and church leadership, and how to deal with false teachings in the church. In this letter, we see Paul, who was advanced in years, passing the torch to a younger Christian leader, encouraging Timothy to "fight the good fight of the faith" (1 Tim. 6:12).

TITUS

Paul wrote this letter to Titus, about AD 64–66. This was likely after Paul had been released from house arrest, but before his second confinement in Rome. Titus was a gentile convert who was in charge of churches on the Island of Crete. He had traveled with Paul years earlier (Gal. 2:1–5). Paul provides instructions about responsible church leadership, correct doctrine, and living in God's grace.

2 TIMOTHY

Paul wrote this second letter to Timothy, about AD 66–67. This was Paul's last epistle. He wrote it while imprisoned in Rome. Paul encourages Timothy to remain faithful in ministry despite hardships. Paul concludes the letter by expressing how he feels deserted by some believers, but Luke is still with him and he looks forward to Timothy visiting him soon (2 Tim. 4:9–18).

1 PETER

Peter wrote this letter to Christians in Asia Minor who faced injustice, about AD 64. This was late in Peter's life, not long before he was executed in Emperor Nero's persecution of Christians. Peter calls Christians to live holy lives and to be encouraged, knowing that Jesus also suffered unjustly in order to bring healing to all.

2 PETER

Peter wrote this letter to Christians, possibly in Asia Minor, about AD 64, soon after 1 Peter was written. He warns Christians about false teachers, encourages believers to grow in their faith, and reminds them of Christ's promised return.

HEBREWS

This letter was written by an unknown author to a Jewish Christian audience facing persecution, about AD 60–69. The message of Hebrews is that Jesus is superior to all things: to angels, the Old Testament prophets, the priesthood, and the sacrificial system. His death on the cross fulfilled the old covenant. Believers enter into his promised land of rest through faith.

JUDE

Jude wrote this letter to Christians everywhere in the latter part of the first century, sometime in the AD 60s–80s, though the exact date of Jude is difficult to determine. Jude may have been the brother of Jesus who is called Judas in Matthew 13:55. This short letter encourages believers to contend for the faith and resist false teachings.

THE APOSTLE JOHN
1, 2 and 3 John; Revelation

John was a young man (probably still a teenager) when he first encountered Jesus, but by the time he wrote his epistles near the end of the first century, he was an elderly man who had seen so much over the years. As one of the original twelve disciples, John had been with Jesus since the beginning of his ministry. John walked with, ate with, and listened to Jesus. He learned from the Master. Yet he also had run in fear for his own life when Jesus was arrested, and he saw his Lord be crucified like a criminal. John was one of the first disciples to see the empty tomb. Later, he witnessed his Lord alive and risen from the grave!

After Christ's ascension, John saw God do miraculous things through the church (Acts 3:1–10). But he also knew the persecution that the church faced and felt the sorrow of losing his own brother to martyrdom (Acts 12:2). Nevertheless, in John's epistles, we see a man assured of eternal life: "I write these things to you who believe in the name of the Son of God so that you may know that you have eternal life" (1 John 5:13). John trusted in God's power to overcome sin and evil: "The one who is in you is greater than the one who is in the world" (1 John 4:4).

John's final writing was the book of Revelation. He received this revelation while exiled for his faith on the island of Patmos. (The Romans would often banish political prisoners to Patmos and surrounding islands.) Here, John received visions from God—just as the ancient prophets Daniel and Ezekiel had received visions while Israel was in exile. Through signs, symbols, and other imagery, God revealed to John what was yet to come and, especially, of the victorious reign of Jesus Christ (Rev. 7:9–10).

Historical evidence suggests that John was eventually released from exile. He lived the remainder of his days with Christians in Ephesus where he died of natural causes, the last of the twelve apostles to exit this world for the next.

1 JOHN

The apostle John wrote this letter to several churches in Asia Minor, about AD 85–95. In this letter, he focuses on God's love through Jesus and our love for one another. Also, some false teachers in the church were claiming that Jesus only *appeared* to be human. John refutes such claims and affirms Jesus' full humanity.

2 JOHN

John wrote this letter to "the lady chosen by God"—possibly an expression meaning "the church"—about AD 85–95. Like John's other epistles, this short letter was probably sent to churches in Asia Minor. John reminds Christians that love means obeying God's instructions and includes being discerning, so that Christians will not be deceived.

3 JOHN

John wrote this letter to Gaius, a Christian in Asia Minor, about AD 85–95. In both 2 John and 3 John, the author calls himself "the elder." In this letter, John commends Gaius for his love, faithfulness, and hospitality. But John also denounces Diotrephes for acting arrogantly, gossiping, and refusing to welcome other believers.

REVELATION

John received this revelation while he was exiled on the island of Patmos for his faith, about AD 95. The book is addressed to seven churches in Asia Minor. Revelation is presented in a series of "sevens," a number of completion: seven messages for seven churches; seven seals, seven bowls, seven trumpets, and so forth. This book reminds believers that even when evil seems strong, God is in control of history. One day, the Lord will renew his creation and dwell with his people for eternity.

AN UNFINISHED STORY

Though Christians have different views about how the end times will unfold, there are some important points of agreement: Christ is coming back again and will judge humanity; the powers of evil are doomed before Christ; and God promises a wonderful future for all who trust in Christ. The final two chapters of the last book of the Bible, Revelation 21–22, give us a glimpse into this future, a time when all things in this world marred by sin and evil will be restored to the life God intended for them since the beginning:

> Then I saw "a new heaven and a new earth," for the first heaven and the first earth had passed away…. And I heard a loud voice from the throne saying, "Look! God's dwelling place is now among the people, and he will dwell with them. They will be his people, and God himself will be with them and be their God. 'He will wipe every tear from their eyes. There will be no more death' or mourning or crying or pain, for the old order of things has passed away." (Rev. 21:1–4)

Many have understood this vision in Revelation to represent a restored garden of Eden. In the first chapter of the Bible, God creates "the heavens and the earth" (Gen. 1:1).

In Revelation, he reveals a new heaven and new earth (Rev. 21:1). Adam and Eve ate from the tree that brought sin into the world instead of the tree of life (Gen. 2:9). In Revelation, the tree of life stands in the middle of the new holy city, bringing healing to the nations (Rev. 22:2).

It's the happy ending to the great story of God. This story is also our story. One day, sin will be abolished and death will be no more. In place of our tears and pain today, there will be infinite joy and life to the full. Lost souls from every "nation, tribe, people and language" will be redeemed (Rev. 7:9). Hard-hearted rebels will become wholehearted worshipers. Those who were dead will live forever, face-to-face with Almighty God himself. Until that day comes, we draw encouragement from the stories of faithful men and women of God who have gone before us.

We join in praise with our great King who says, "I am making everything new!" (Rev. 21:5).

CHRONOLOGICAL READING GUIDE

BEGINNINGS

Creation
- ❏ Gen. 1–2

A Fallen World
- ❏ Gen. 3–11

Story of Job
- ❏ Job 1–42

THE PATRIARCHS

Abraham and Sarah
- ❏ Gen. 12–24

Isaac and Jacob
- ❏ Gen. 25–36

Joseph
- ❏ Gen. 37–50

THE EXODUS

Moses
- ❏ Ex. 1–4

The Exodus
- ❏ Ex. 5–18

At Mount Sinai
- ❏ Ex.19–40
- ❏ Lev. 1–27
- ❏ Num. 1–9

Wilderness
- ❏ Num. 10–36

Moses's Final Sermons
- ❏ Deut. 1–34

PROMISED LAND

Conquest of Canaan
- ❏ Josh. 1–24

The Judges
- ❏ Judg. 1–21

Story of Ruth
- ❏ Ruth 1–4

UNITED KINGDOM

Samuel, Saul, David
- ❏ 1 Sam. 1–31
- ❏ 1 Chron. 1–10

King David
- ❏ 2 Sam. 1–24
- ❏ 1 Chron. 11–29
- ❏ 1 Kings 1–2

Psalms of Israel
- ❏ Ps. 1–150

King Solomon
- ❏ 1 Kings 3–11
- ❏ 2 Chron. 1–9

Wisdom and Poetry
- ❏ Prov. 1–31
- ❏ Song. 1–8
- ❏ Eccl. 1–12

DIVIDED KINGDOM

Kings of Israel & Judah
- ❏ 1 Kings 12–22
- ❏ 2 Kings 1–16
- ❏ 2 Chron. 10–28

Prophets
- ❏ Jonah 1–4
- ❏ Amos 1–9
- ❏ Hosea 1–14
- ❏ Micah 1–7
- ❏ Isaiah 1–66

Fall of Israel
- ❏ 2 Kings 17

Final Kings of Judah
- ❏ 2 Kings 18–24
- ❏ 2 Chron. 29–35

Prophets
- ❏ Nahum 1–3
- ❏ Zeph. 1–3
- ❏ Jer. 1–52
- ❏ Hab. 1–3
- ❏ Obad.

Fall of Judah
- ❏ 2 Kings 25
- ❏ 2 Chron. 36
- ❏ Lam 1–5

EXILE AND RETURN

Prophets of the Exile
- ❏ Dan. 1–12
- ❏ Ezek. 1–48

1st Return
- ❏ Ezra 1–6

Prophets
- ❏ Hag. 1–2
- ❏ Zech. 1–14

Story of Esther
- ❏ Est. 1–10

2nd Return
- ❏ Ezra 7–10

3rd Return
- ❏ Neh. 1–13

Prophets
- ❏ Mal. 1–4
- ❏ Joel 1–3

LIFE OF JESUS

Birth of Christ
- ❏ Matt. 1–2
- ❏ Luke 1–2

Early Ministry
- ❏ Matt. 3–4
- ❏ Mark 1
- ❏ Luke 3–4
- ❏ John 1–4

Teachings
- ❏ Matt. 5–20
- ❏ Mark 2–10
- ❏ Luke 5–18
- ❏ John 5–11

Journey to the Cross
- ❏ Matt. 21–27
- ❏ Mark 11–15
- ❏ Luke 19–23
- ❏ John 12–19

Resurrection and Ascension
- ❏ Matt. 28
- ❏ Mark 16
- ❏ Luke 24
- ❏ John 20–21
- ❏ Acts 1

THE APOSTLES

Pentecost
- ❏ Acts 2–3

First Christians
- ❏ Acts 4–8

Paul's Conversion
- ❏ Acts 9

Peter's Mission
- ❏ Acts 10–12

James's Epistle
- ❏ James 1–5

1st Journey
- ❏ Acts 13–14
- ❏ Gal. 1–6

2nd Journey
- ❏ Acts 15–18
- ❏ 1 Thess. 1–5
- ❏ 2 Thess. 1–3

3rd Journey
- ❏ Acts 19–21
- ❏ 1 Cor. 1–16
- ❏ 2 Cor. 1–13
- ❏ Rom. 1–16

Journey to Rome
- ❏ Acts 22–28

Epistles from Rome
- ❏ Eph. 1–6
- ❏ Phil. 1–4
- ❏ Col. 1–4
- ❏ Philem.

AFTER ACTS

Paul's Latter Epistles
- ❏ 1 Tim. 1–6
- ❏ Titus 1–3
- ❏ 2 Tim. 1–4

Other Epistles
- ❏ 1 Peter 1–5
- ❏ 2 Peter 1–3
- ❏ Heb. 1–13
- ❏ Jude

John's Writings
- ❏ 1 John 1–5
- ❏ 2 John
- ❏ 3 John
- ❏ Rev. 1–22

MADE EASY

by Rose Publishing

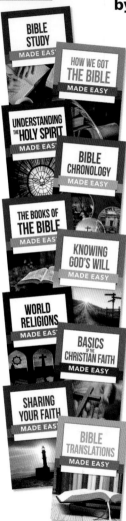

BIBLE STUDY MADE EASY
A step-by-step guide to studying God's Word

HOW WE GOT THE BIBLE MADE EASY
Key events in the history of the Bible

UNDERSTANDING THE HOLY SPIRIT MADE EASY
Who the Holy Spirit is and what he does

BIBLE CHRONOLOGY MADE EASY
Bible characters and events in the order they happened

THE BOOKS OF THE BIBLE MADE EASY
Quick summaries of all 66 books of the Bible

KNOWING GOD'S WILL MADE EASY
Answers to tough questions about God's will

WORLD RELIGIONS MADE EASY
30 religions and how they compare to Christianity

BASICS OF THE CHRISTIAN FAITH MADE EASY
Key Christian beliefs and practices

SHARING YOUR FAITH MADE EASY
How to share the gospel

BIBLE TRANSLATIONS MADE EASY
Compares 20 popular Bible versions

www.hendricksonrose.com